Pattern Play

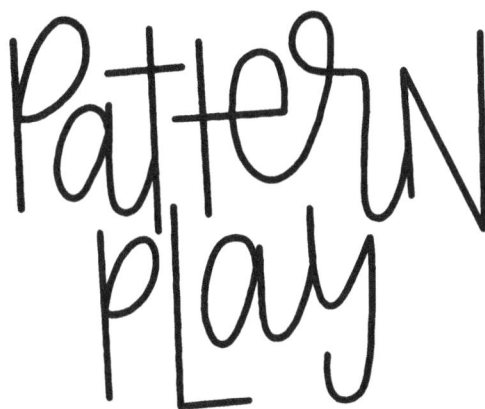

COLORING BOOK

by Tara Larson Nearents
of Rad and Happy

WWW.RADANDHAPPY.COM

Pattern Play Coloring Book
©2016 Rad And Happy
Huntington Beach, CA 92648

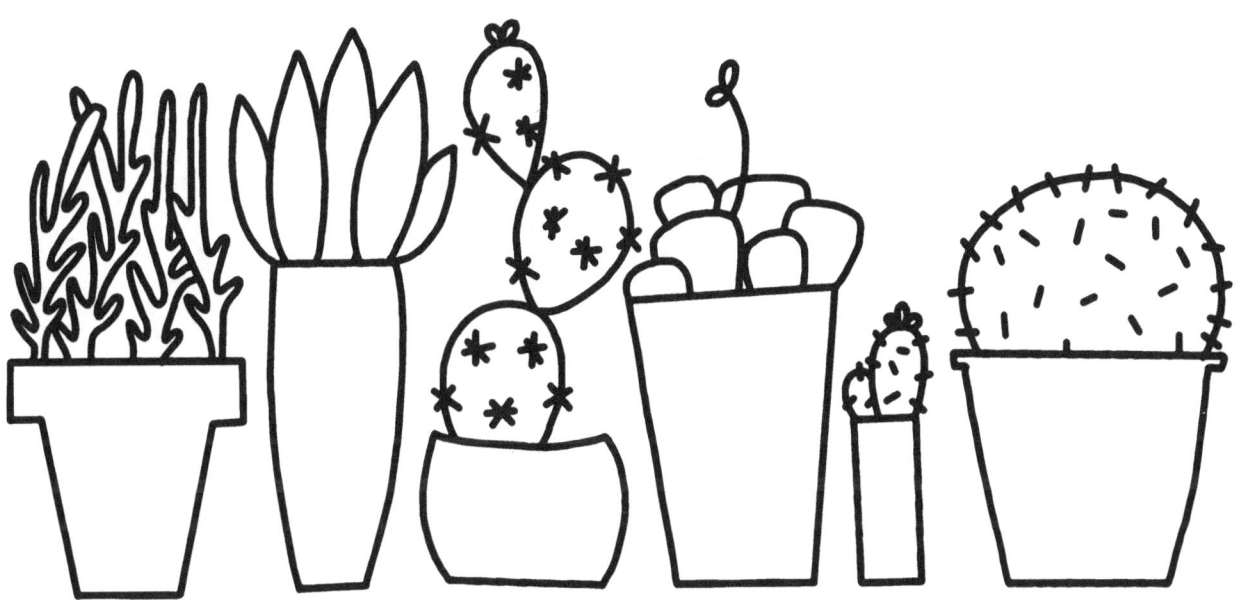

USE THIS PAGE TO TEST MATERIALS

Psst.. Feel free to share the love on Instagram via
@radandhappy and #radandhappycoloring
to possibly have your work featured and connect with
other good looking coloring masters like yourself.

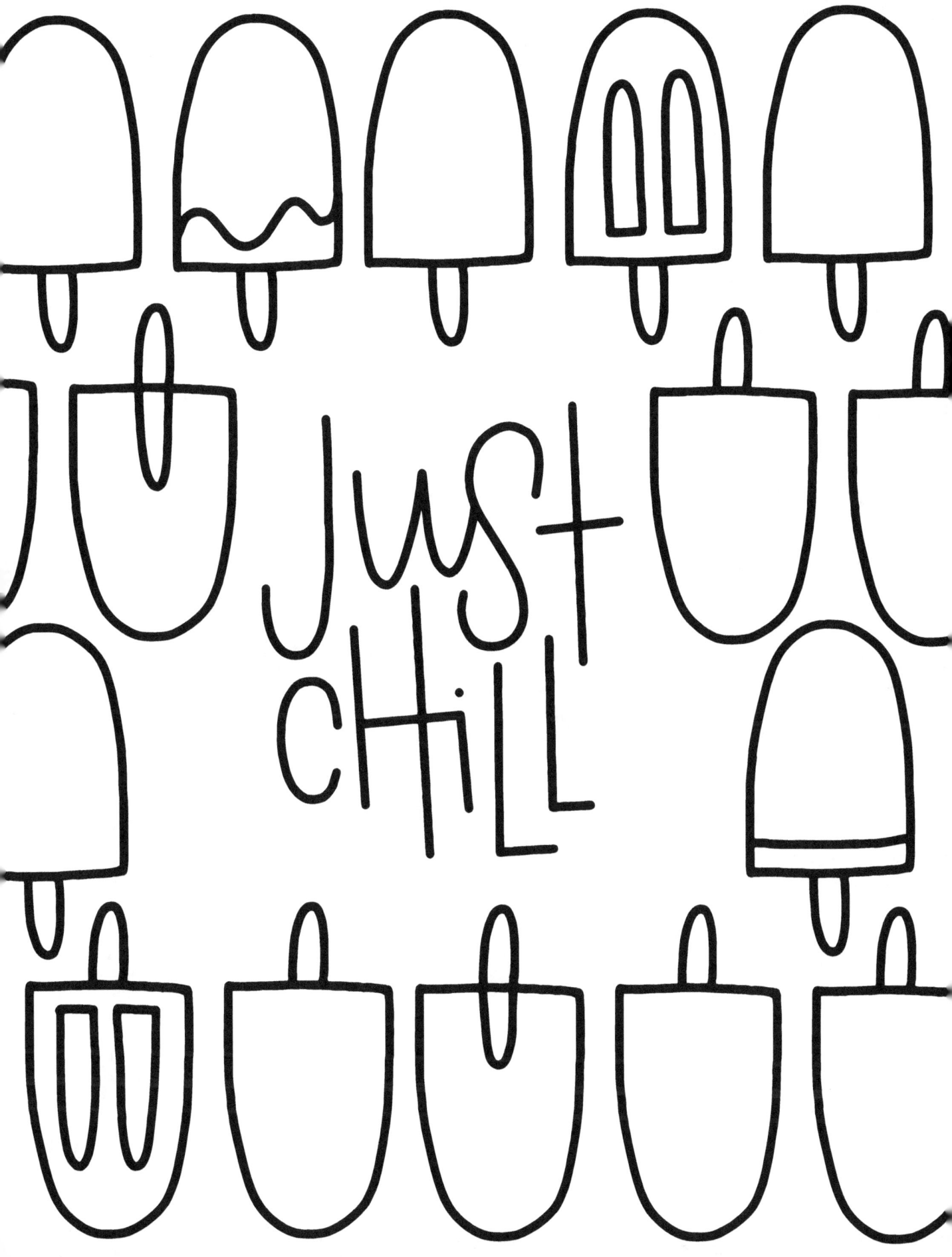

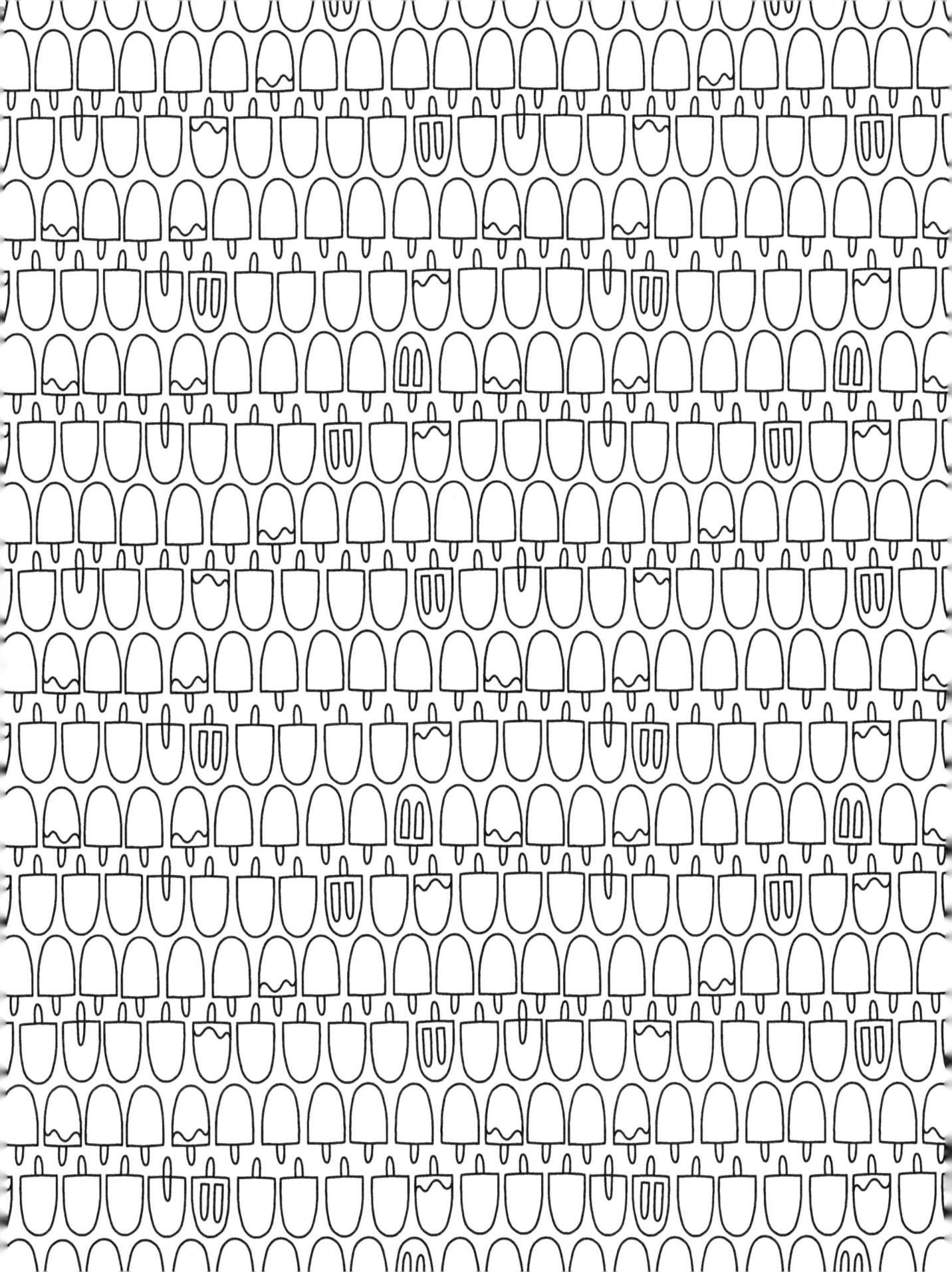

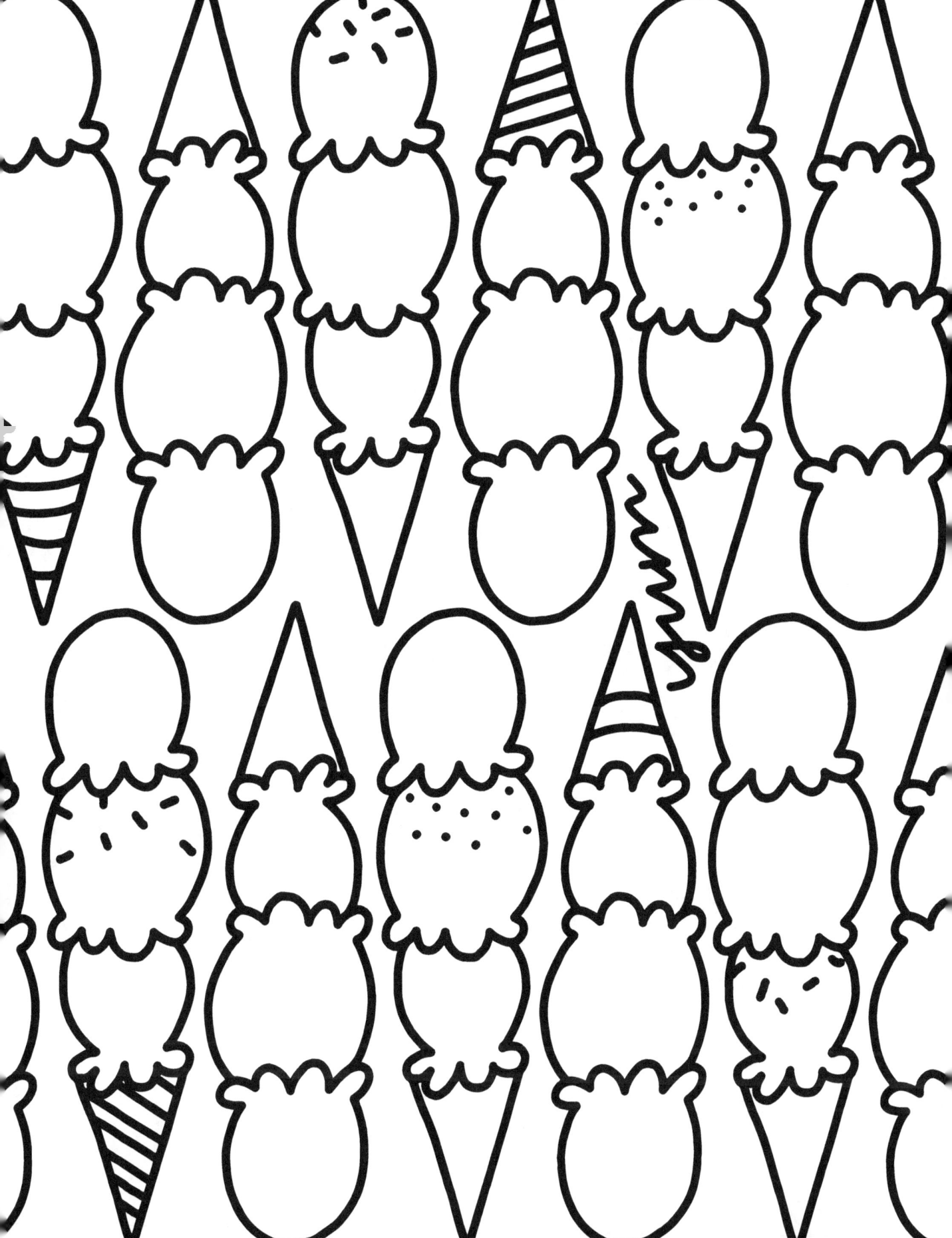

DANG, YOU'RE REALLY GOOD AT THIS

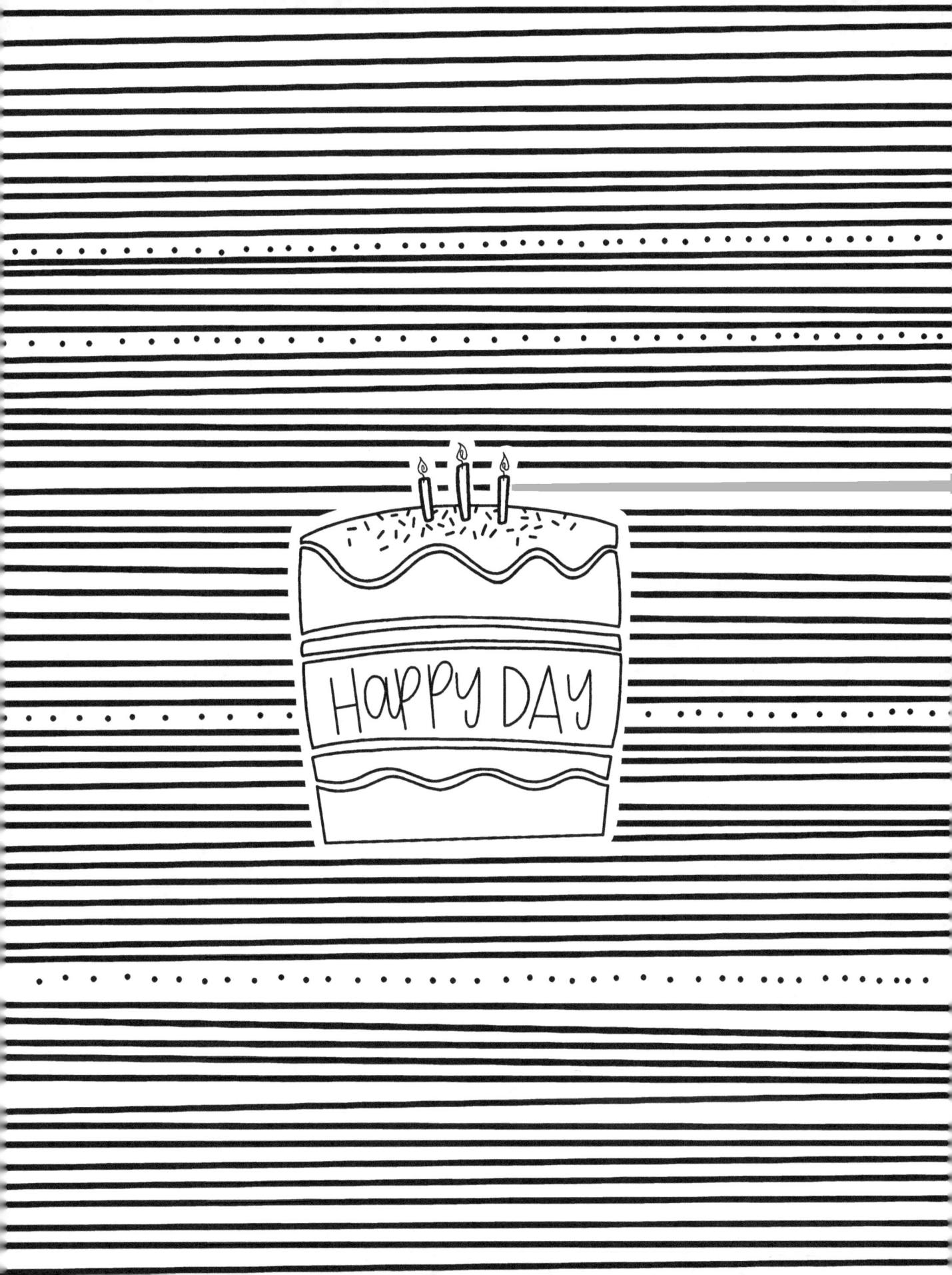

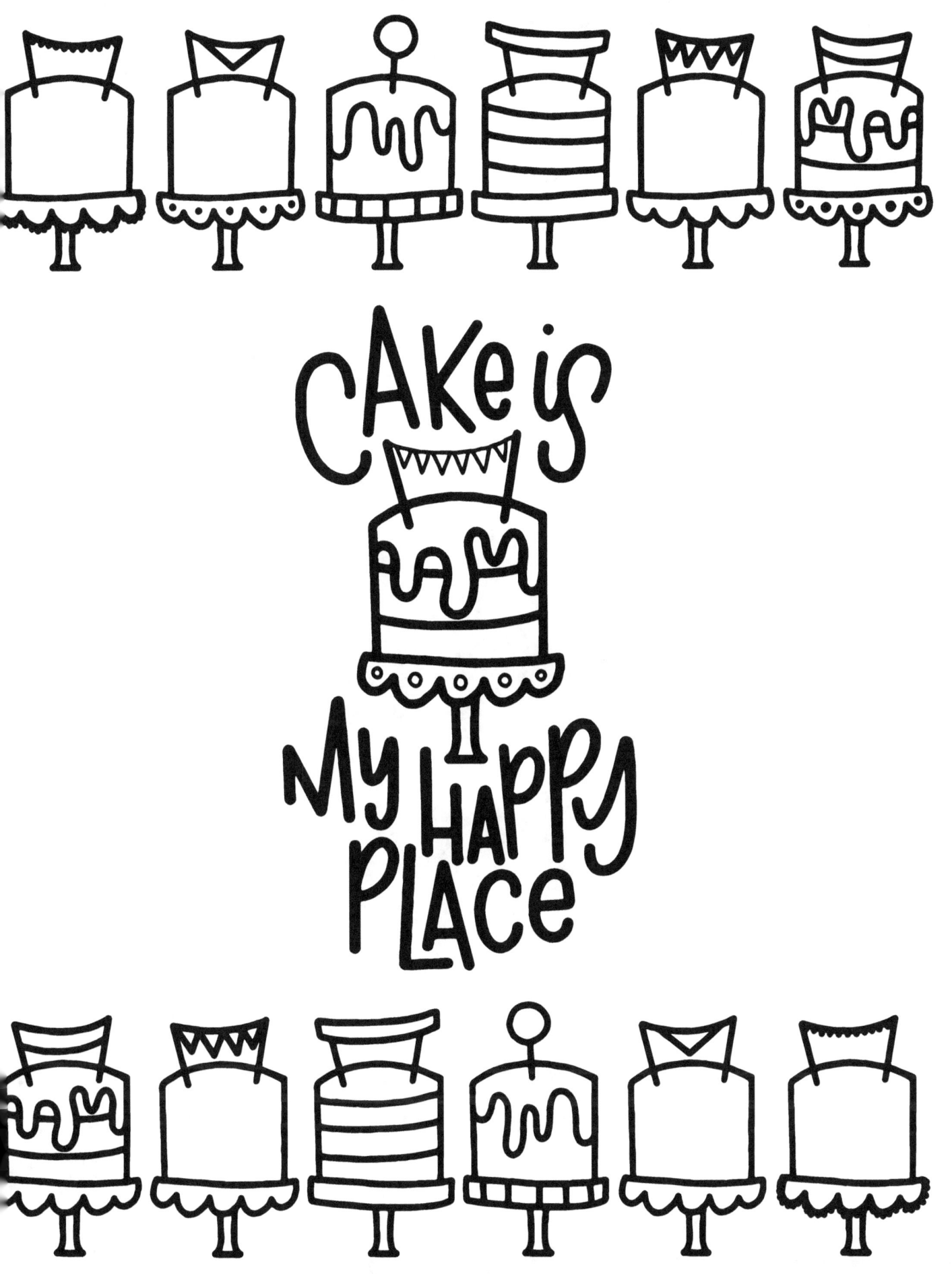

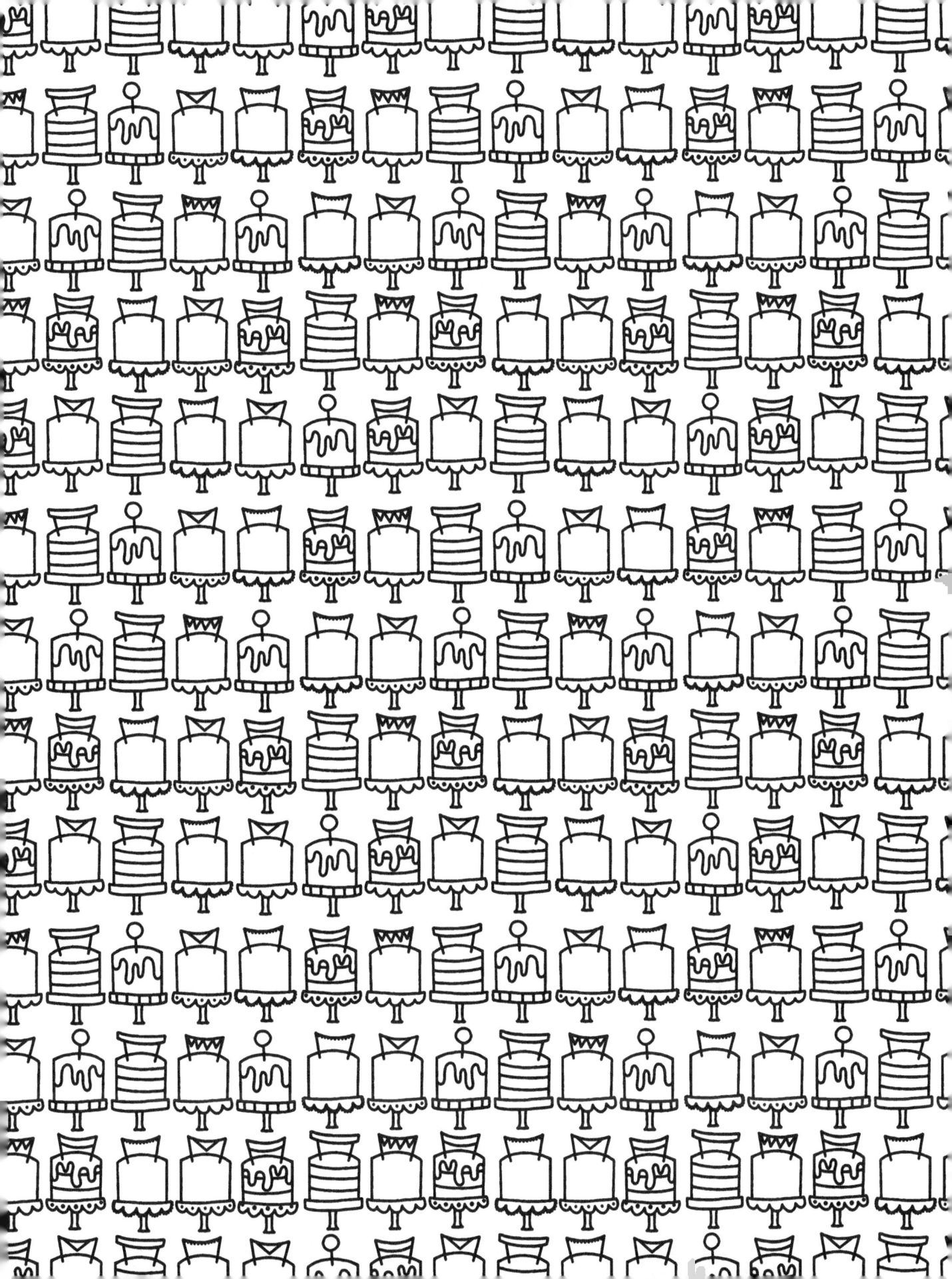

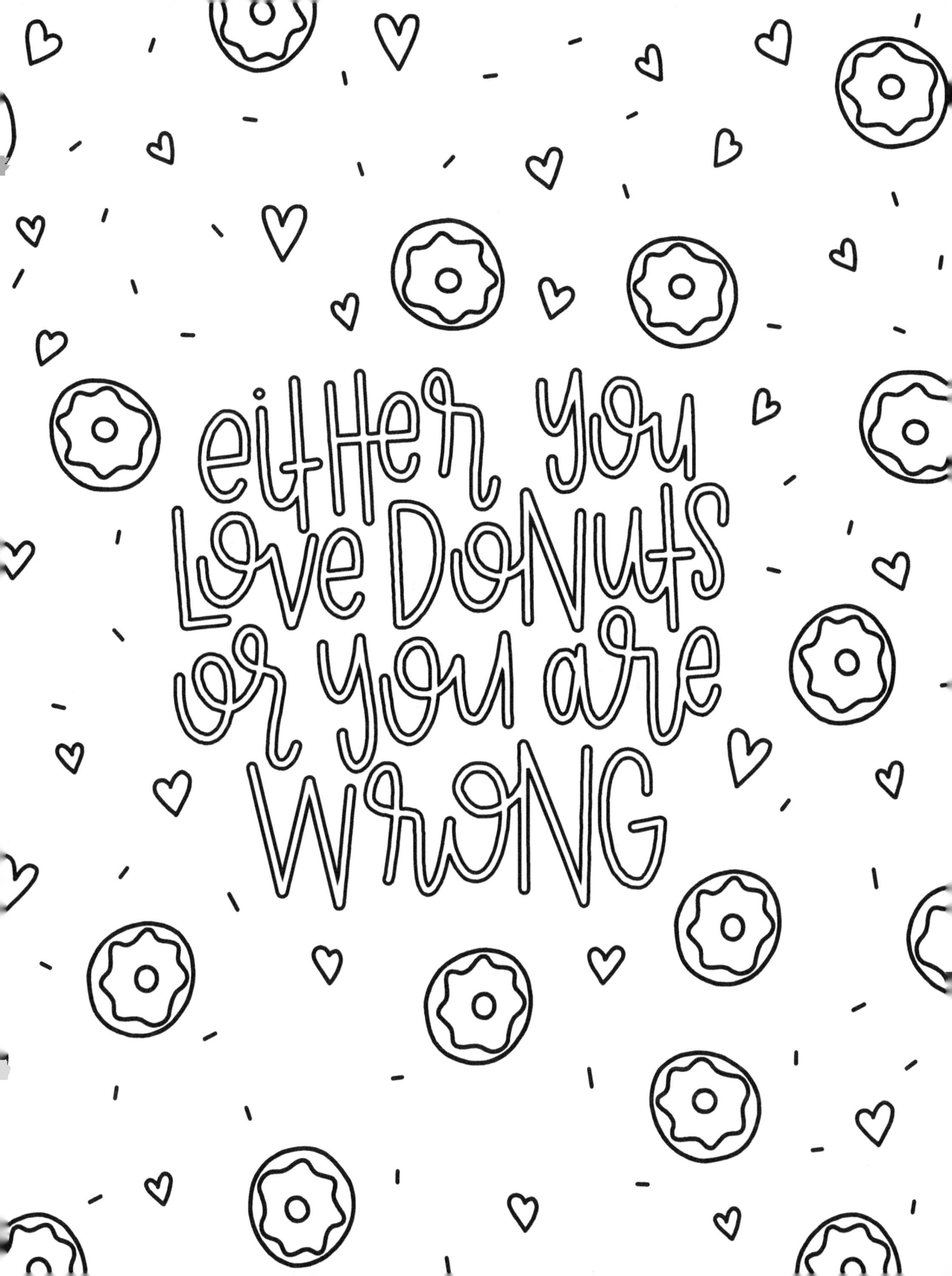

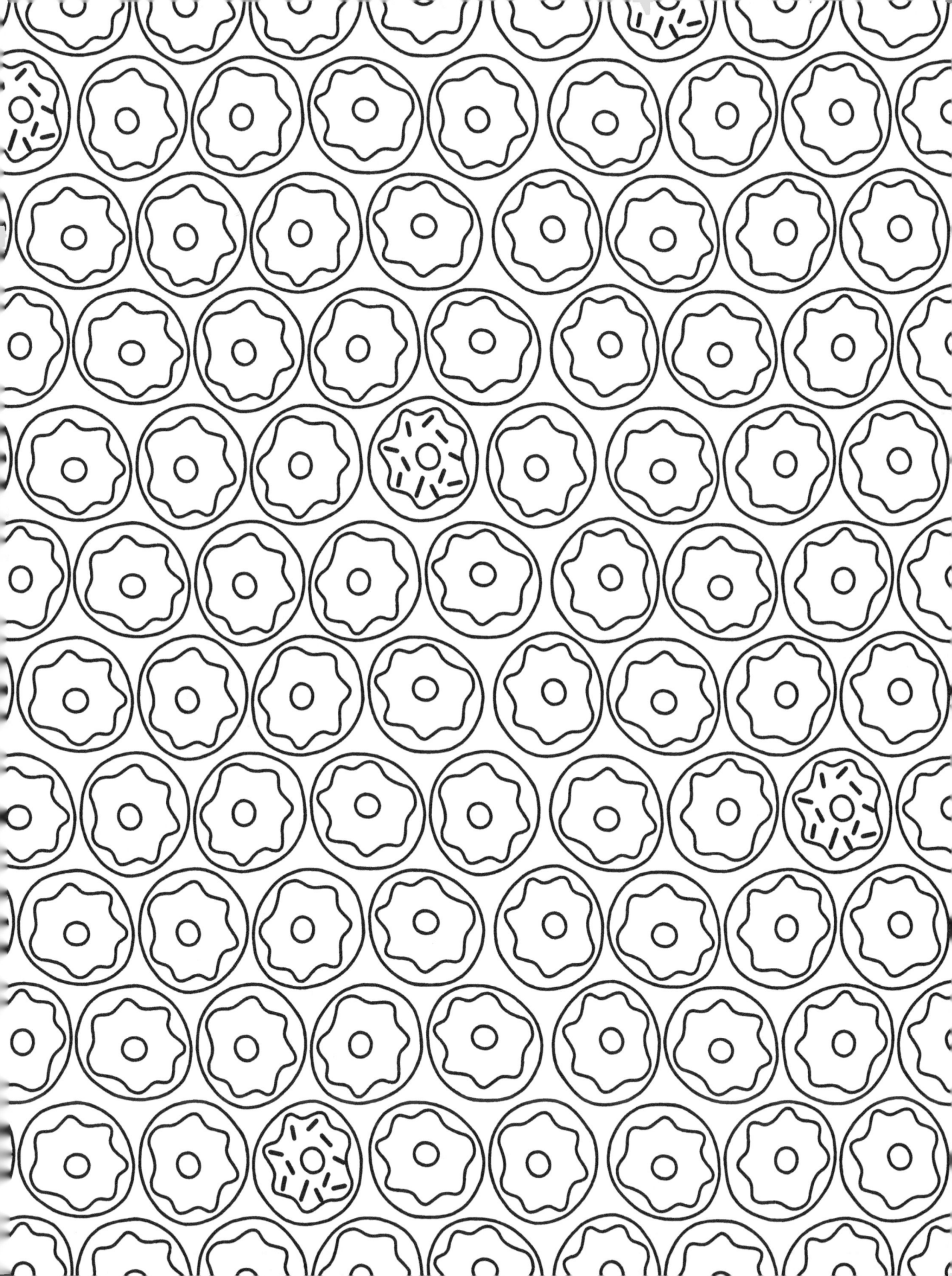

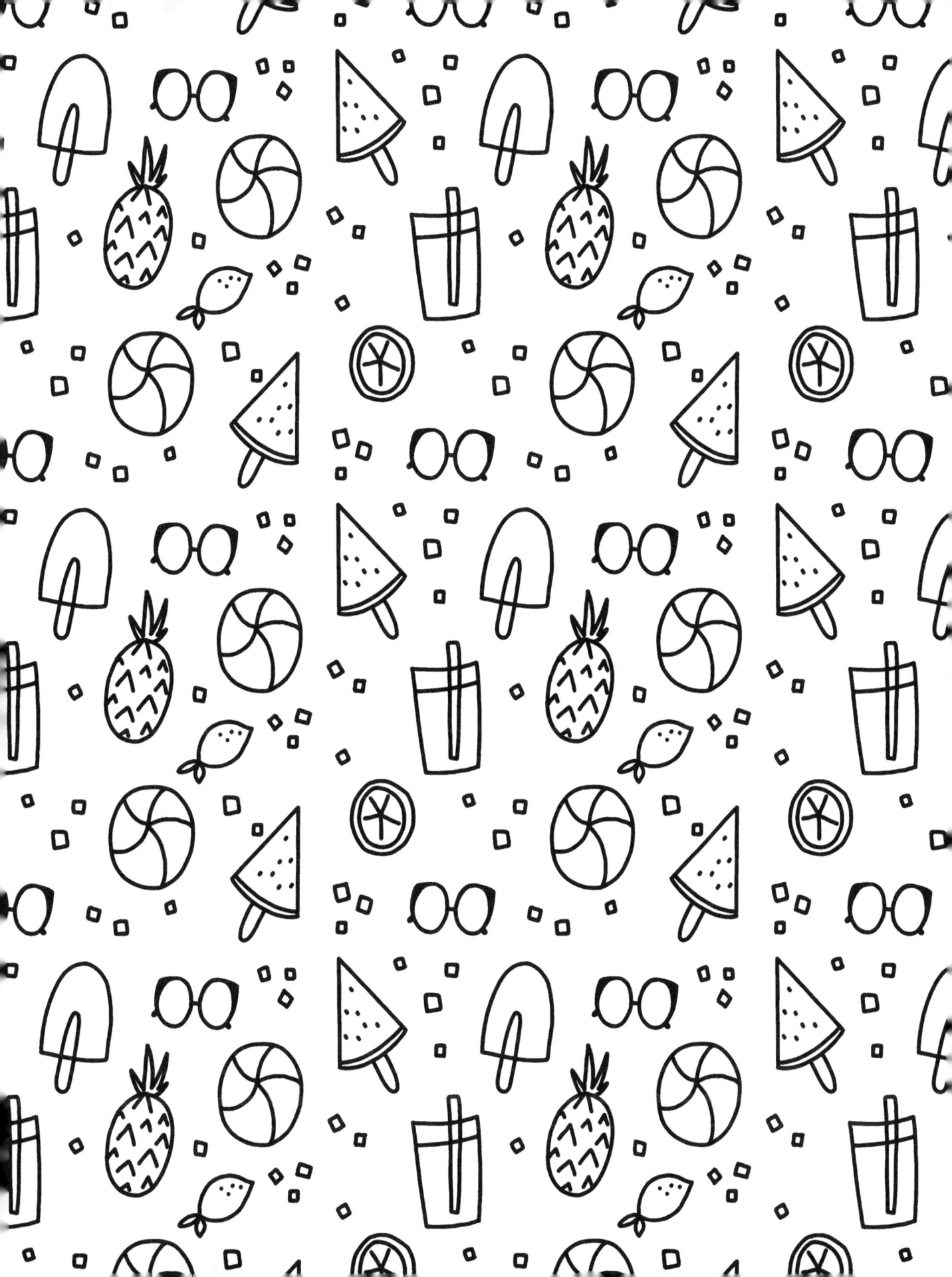

tHiS SaLaD. TaSteS LiKe i WoulD rather Be fat

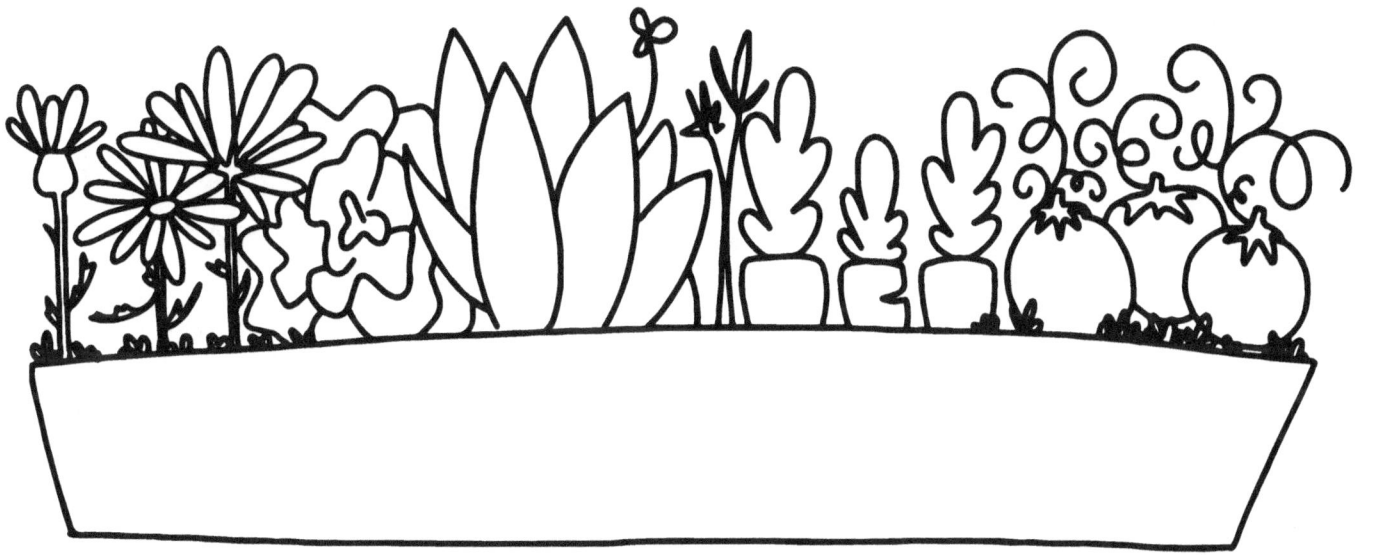

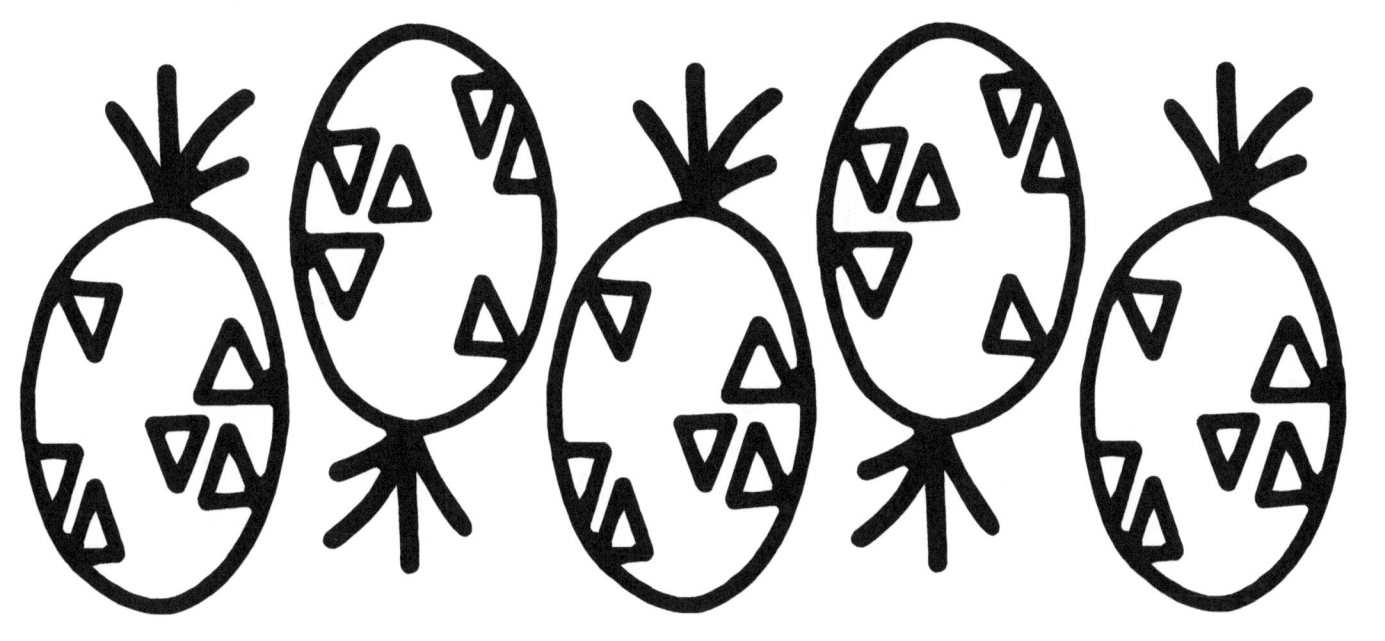

you're sweet

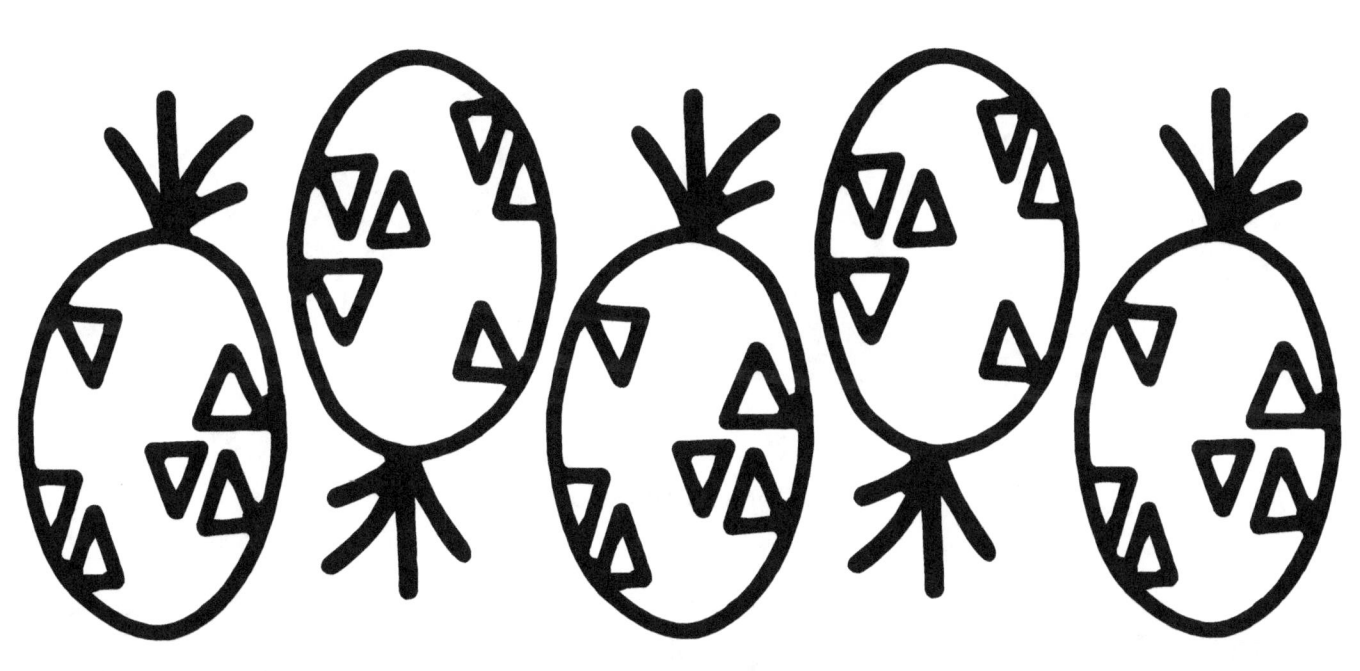

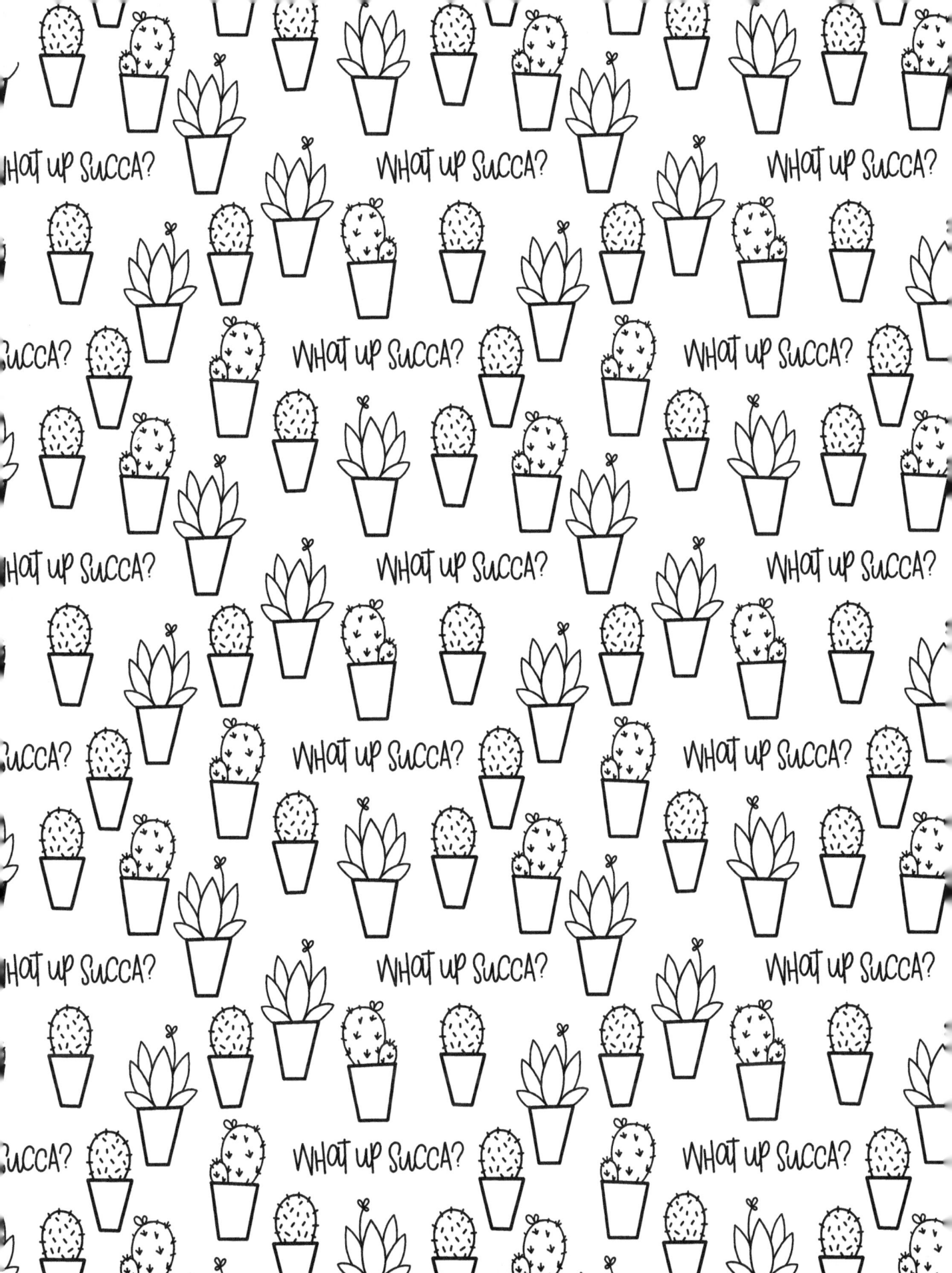

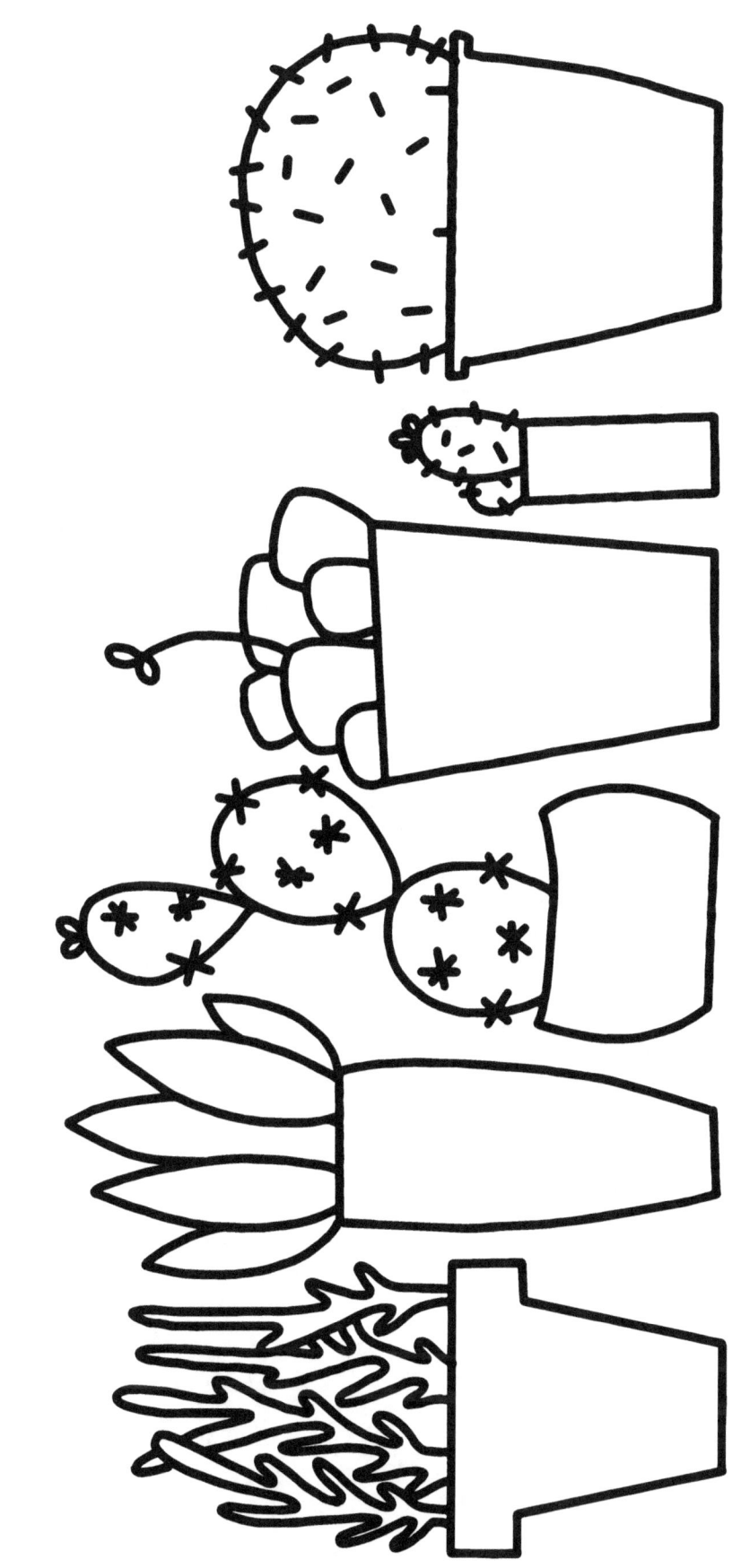

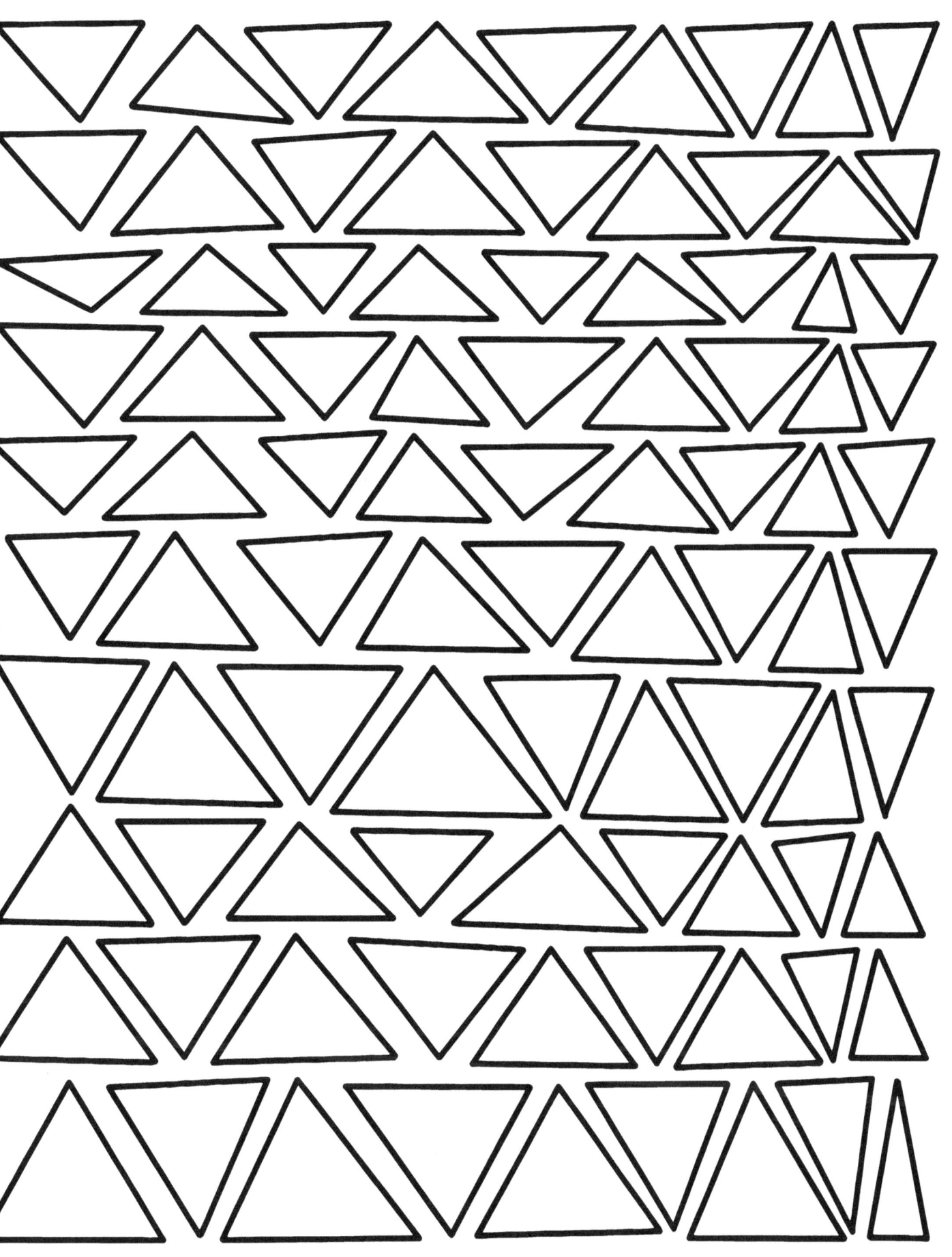

OK LOVE WHERE YOU'RE GOING WITH THIS

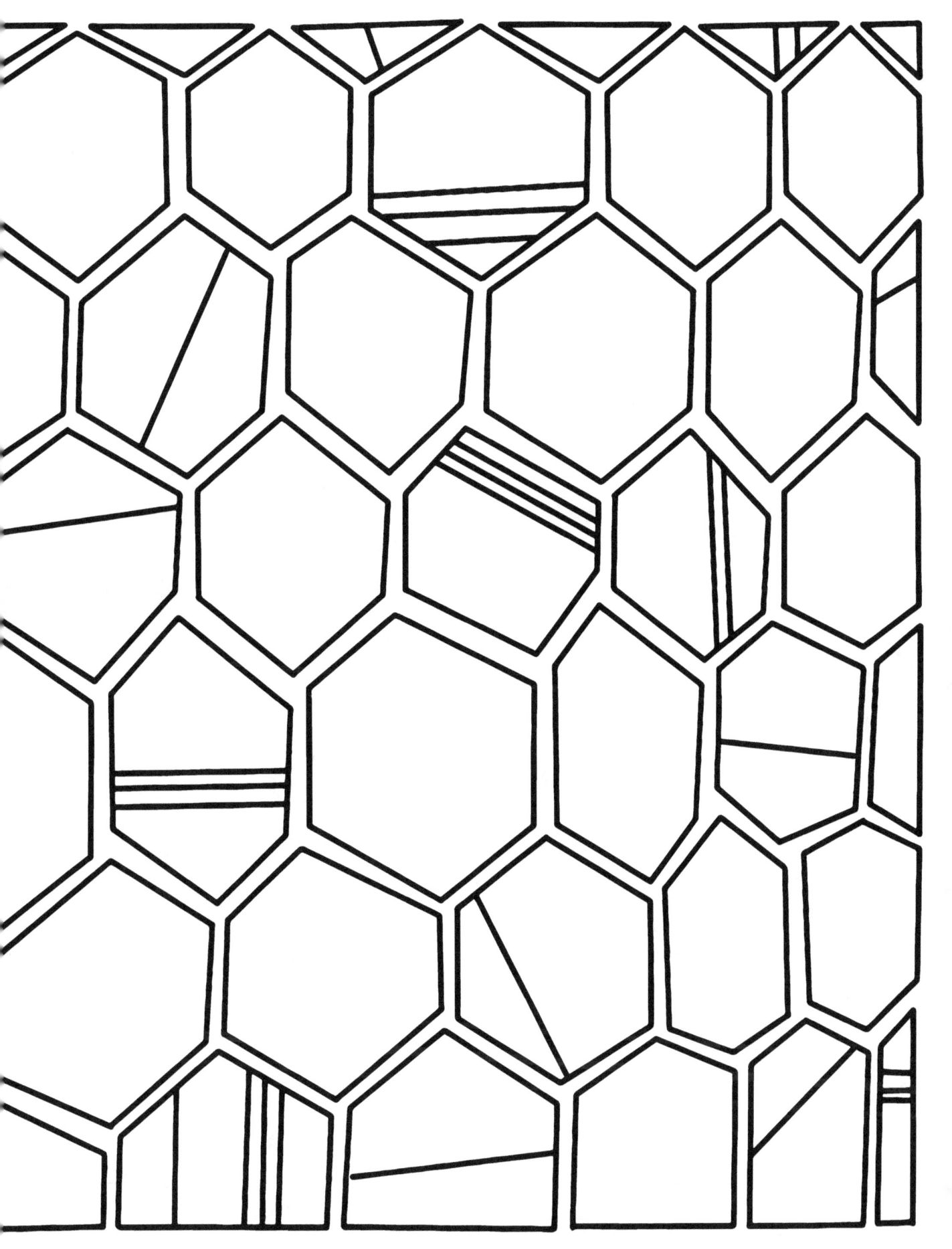

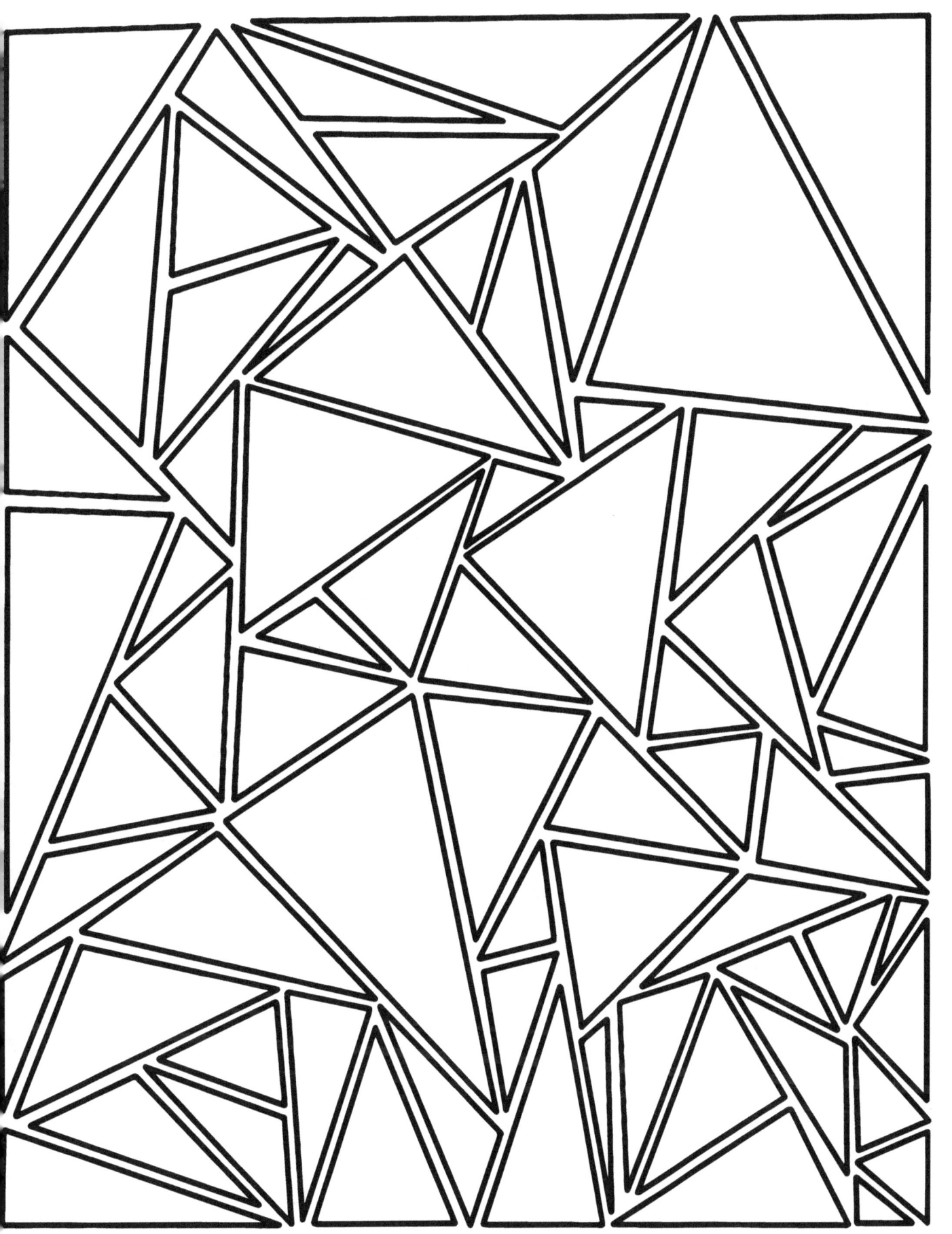

YOU ARE ROCKING THIS

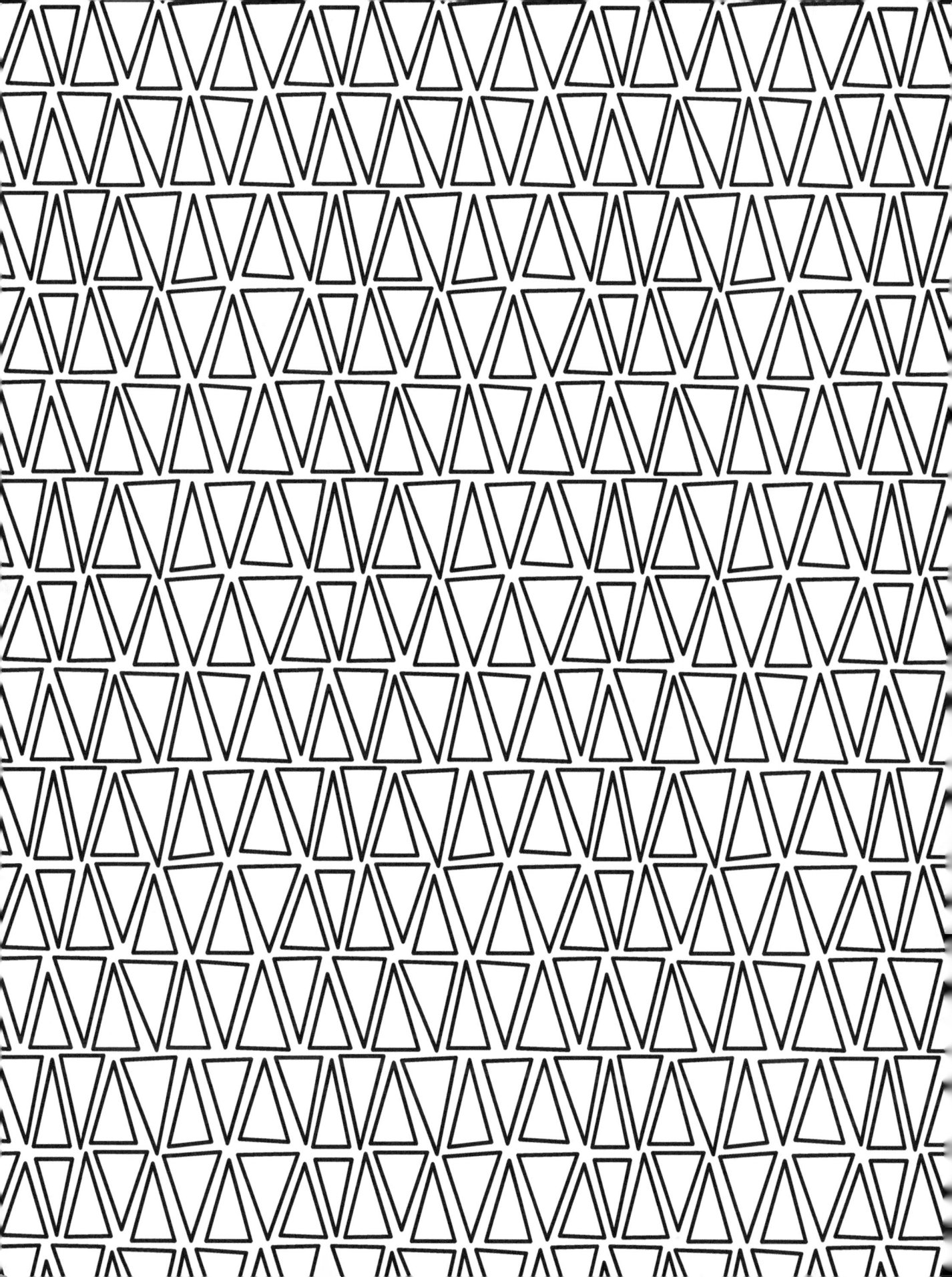

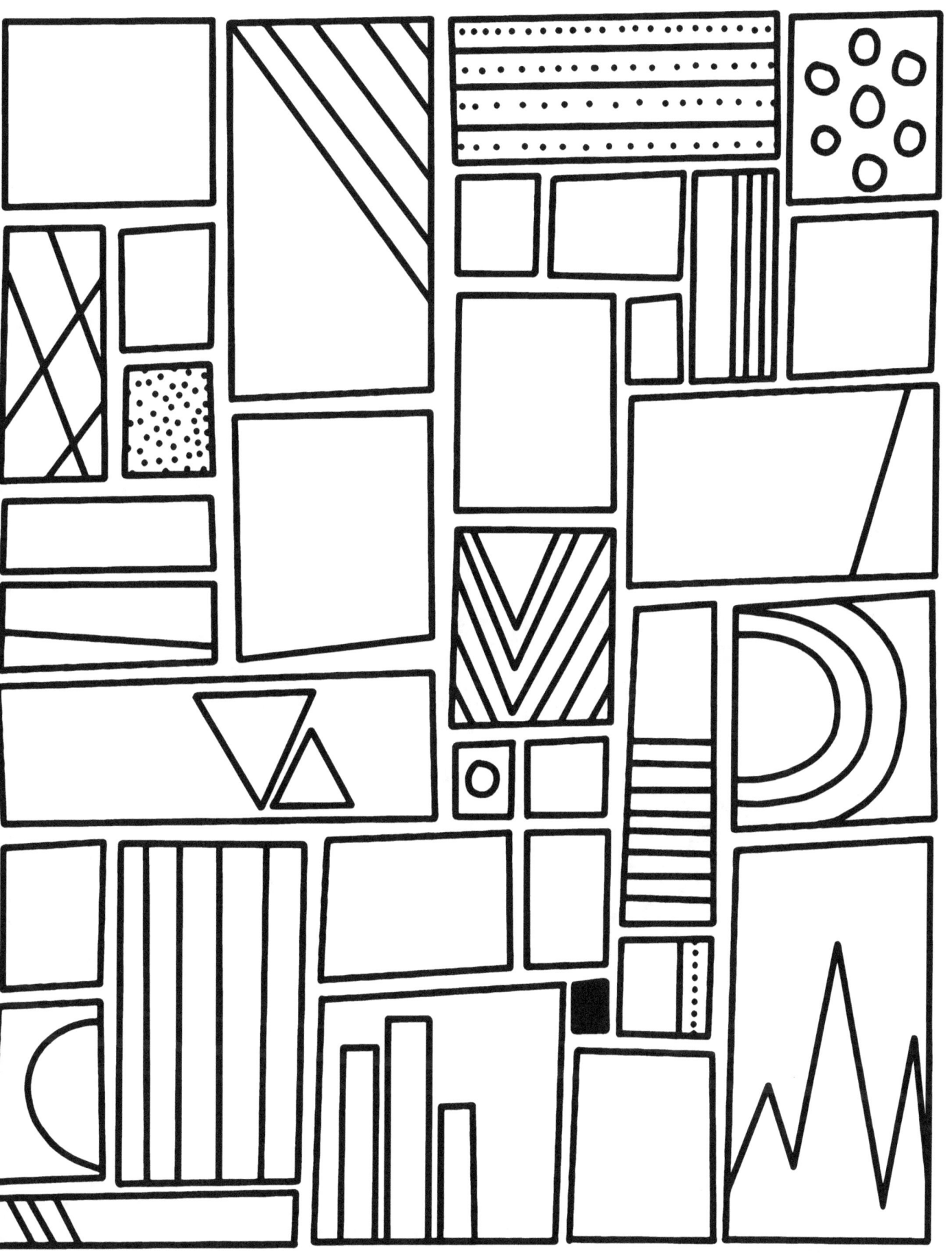

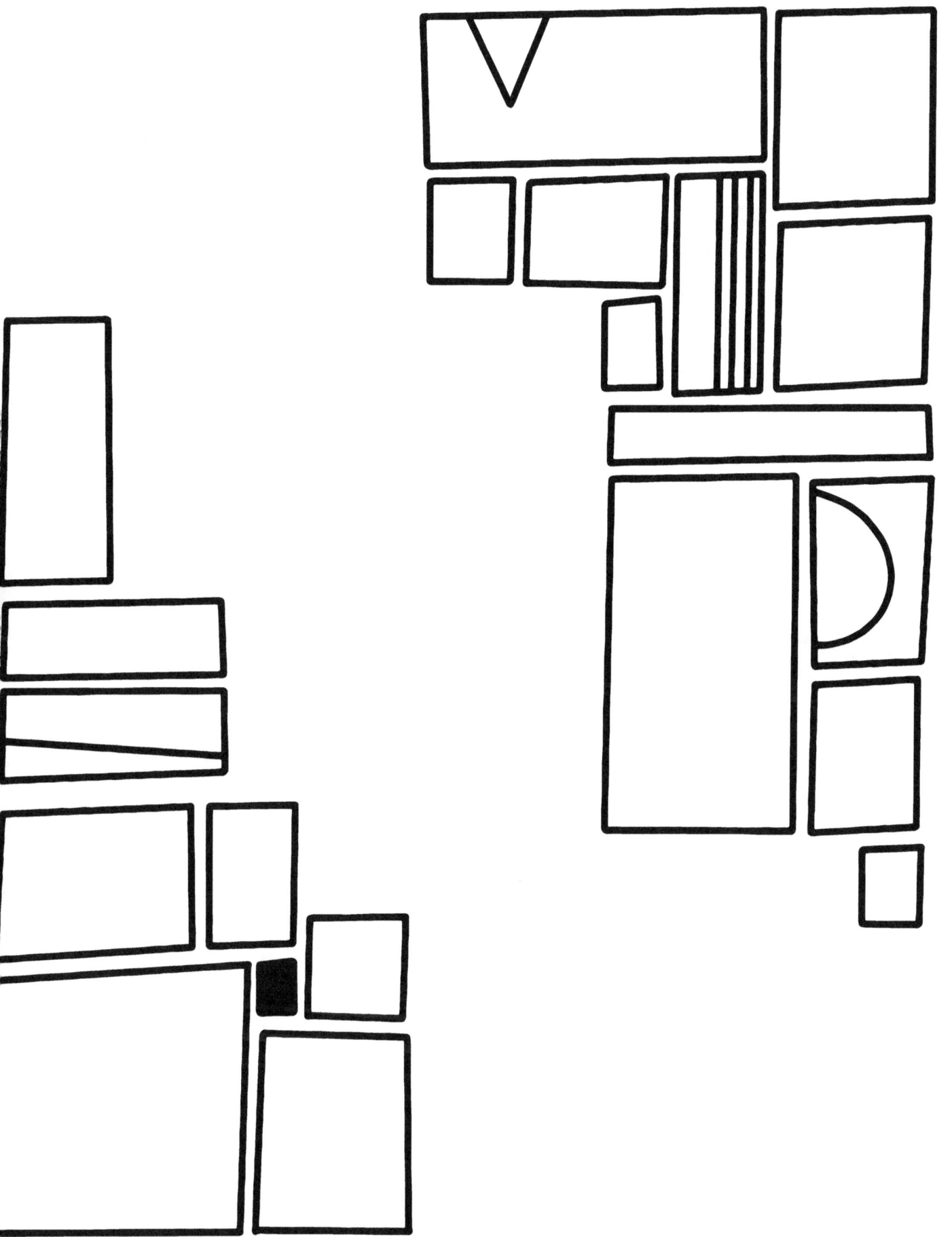

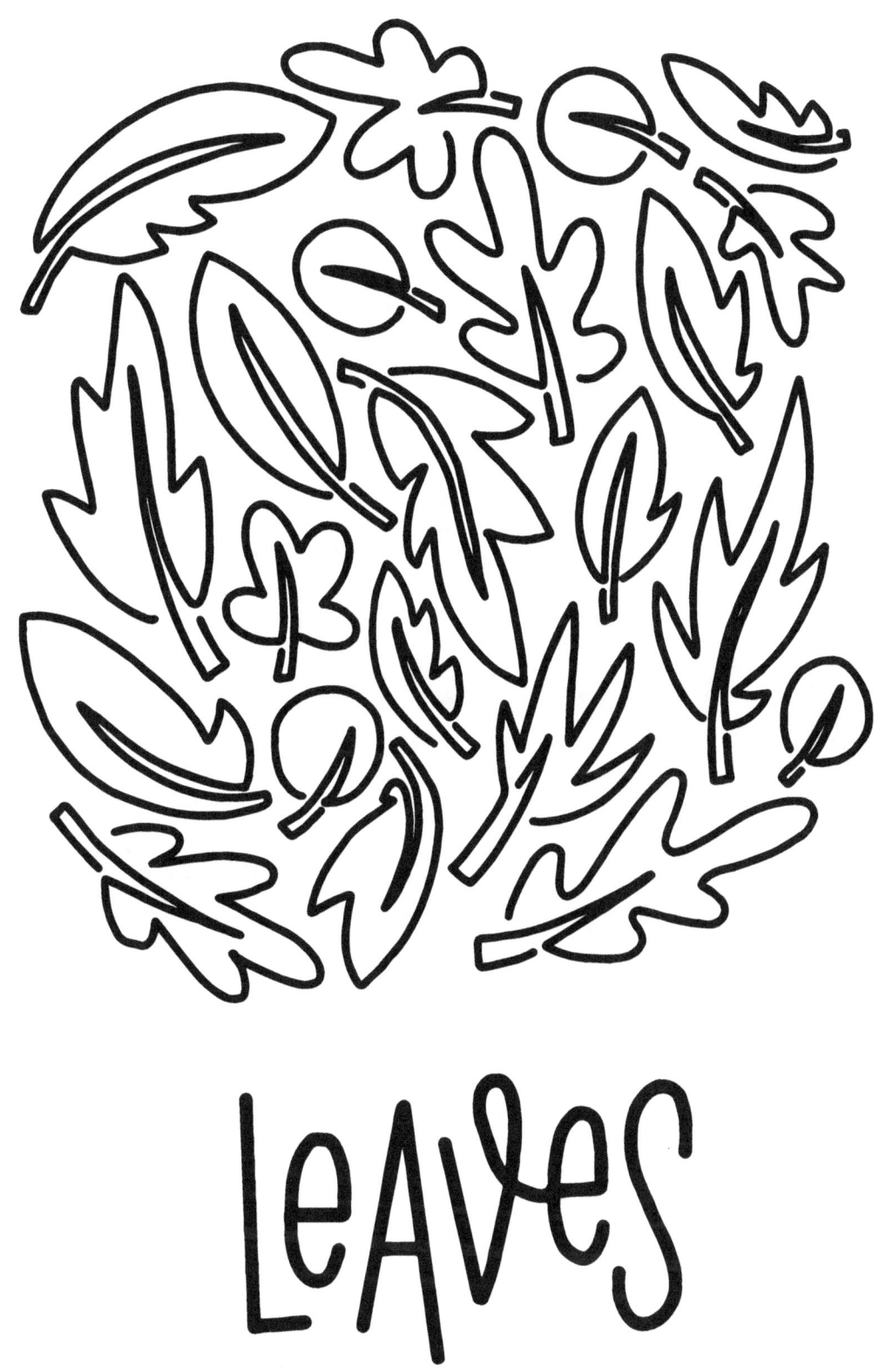

LEAVES

YOU'RE AS GLORIOUS AS A TALL STACK OF PANCAKES

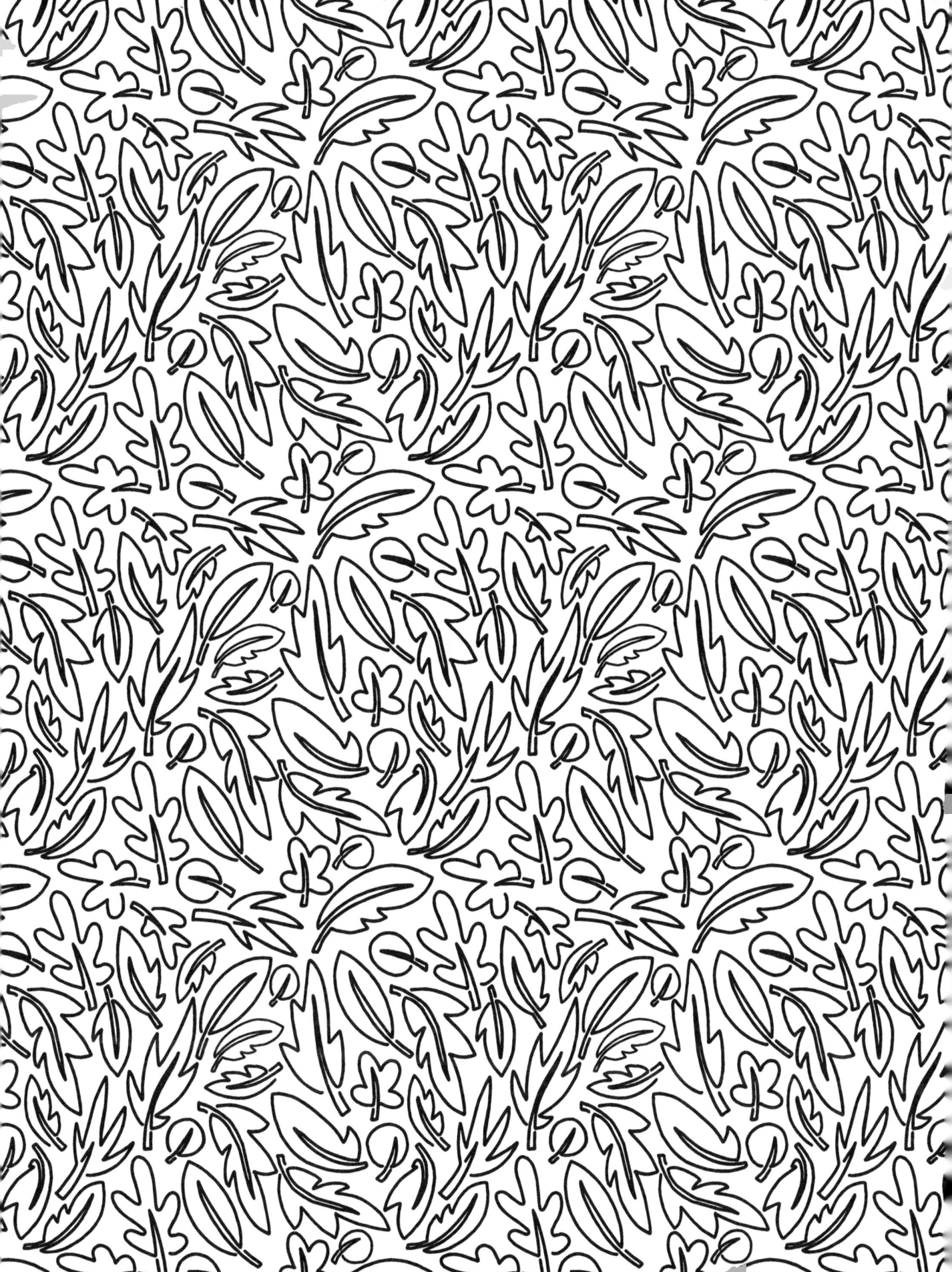

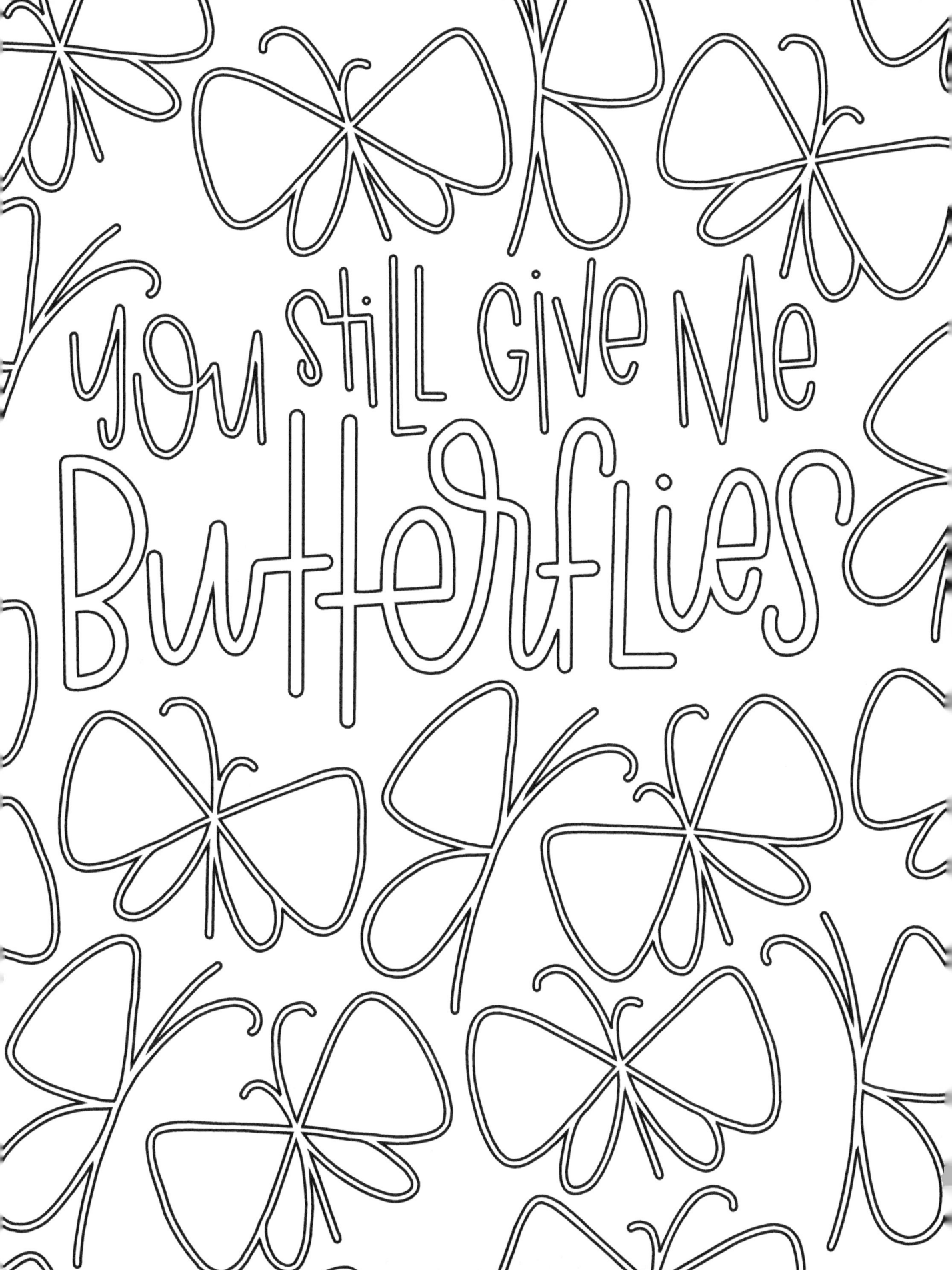

YOU ARE FANTASTICALLY FANTASTIC

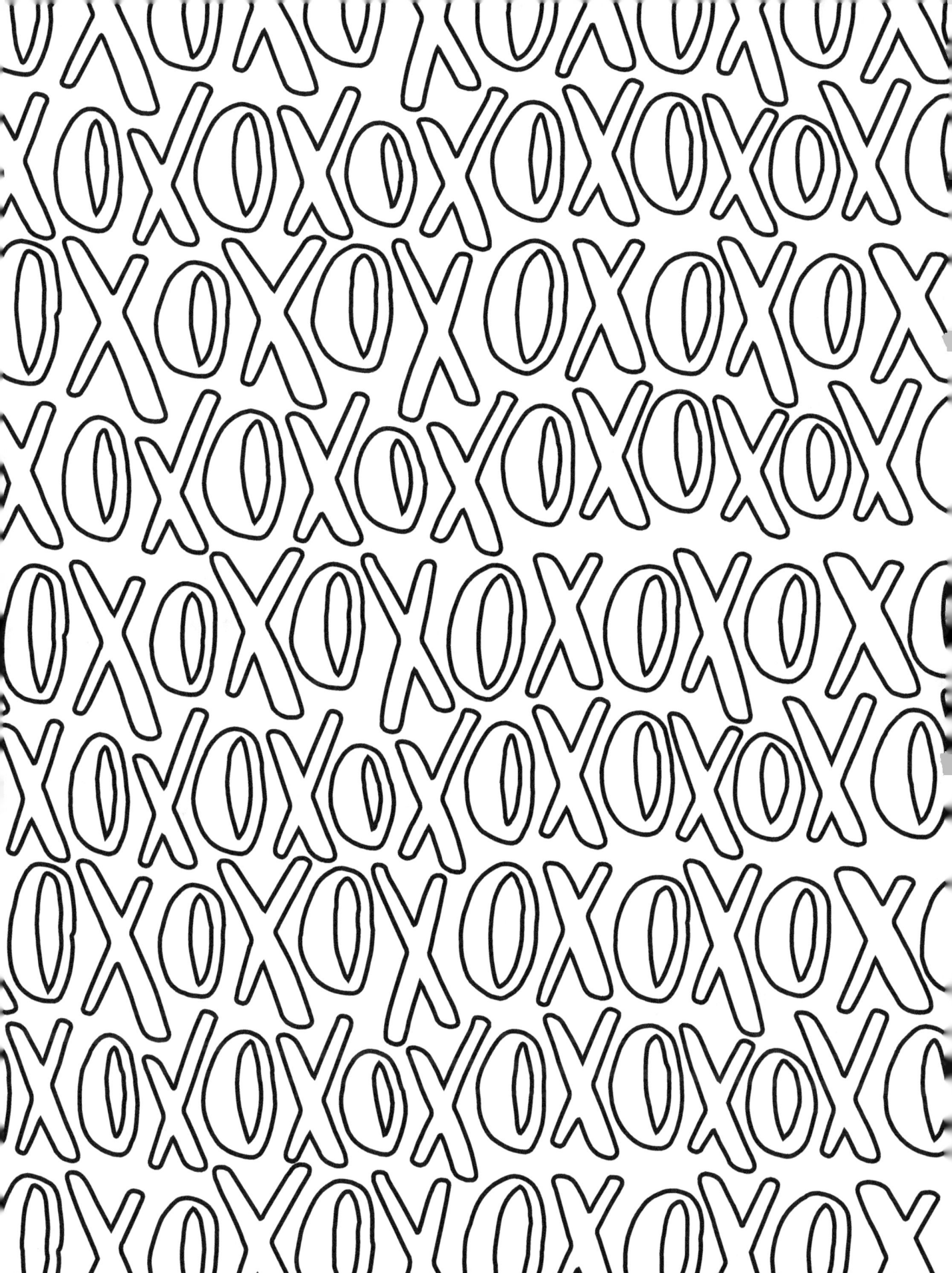

From the
tiniest acorn
grows the
mighty oak

IT'S NUTS HOW TALENTED YOU ARE

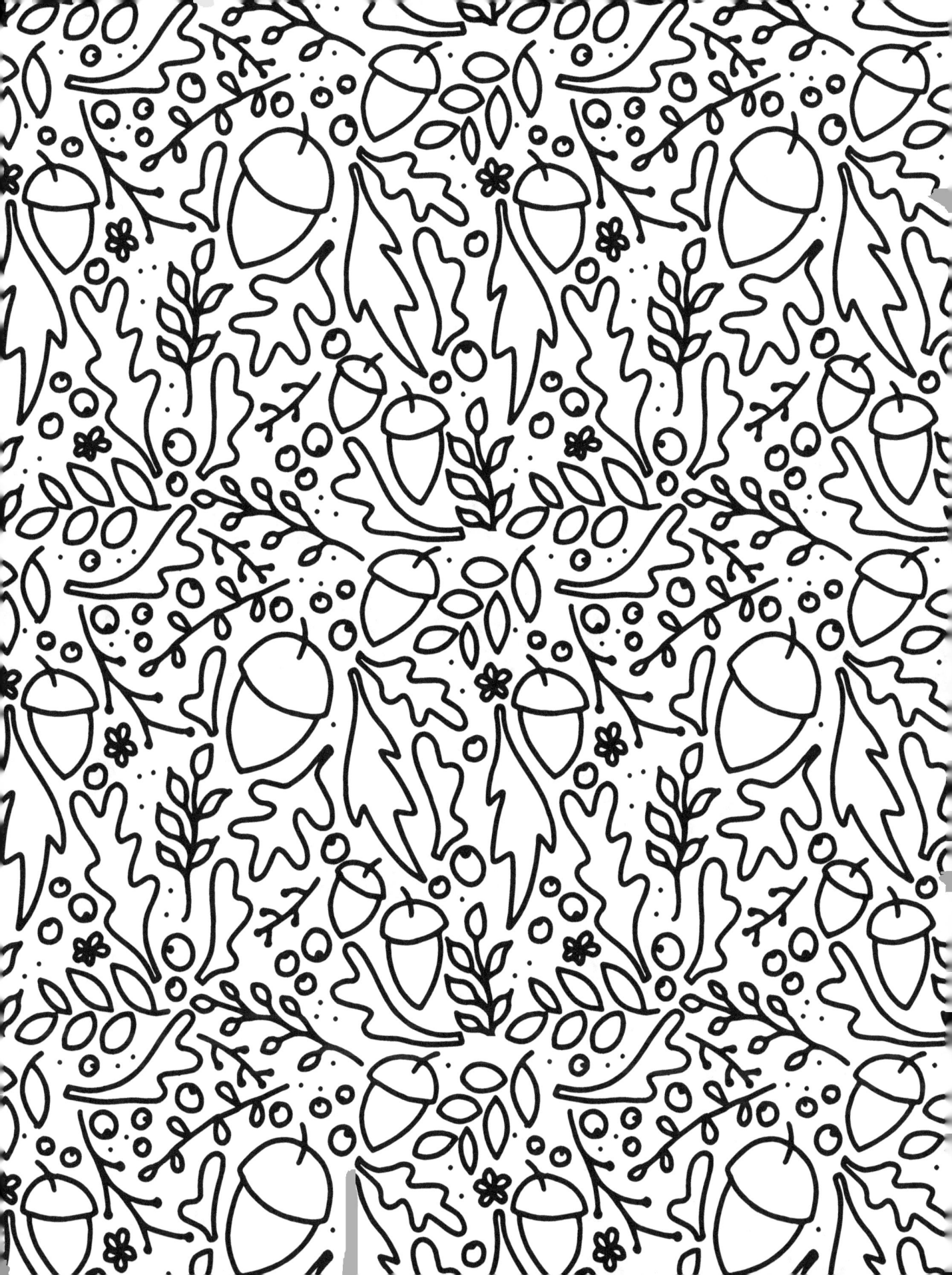

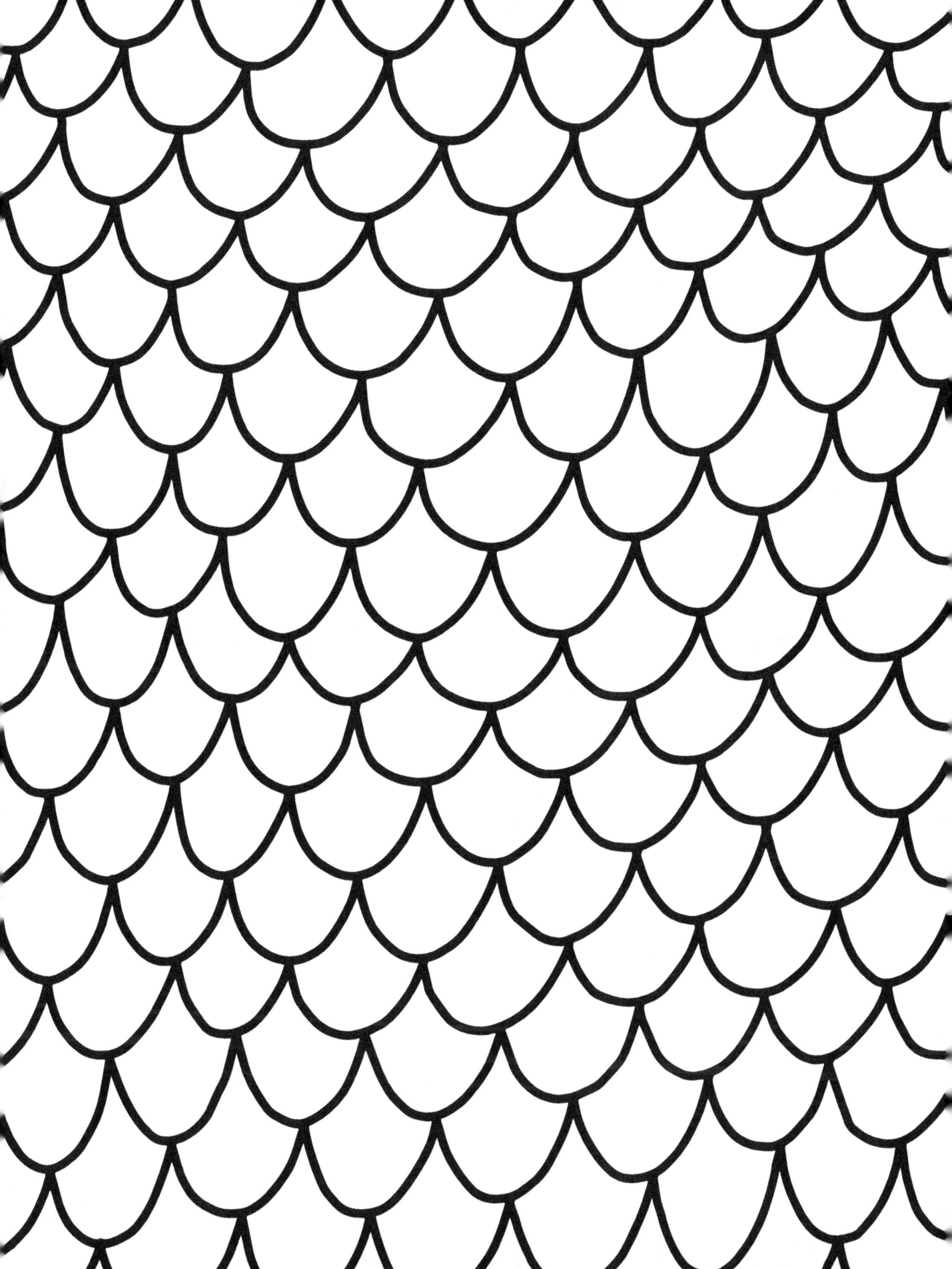

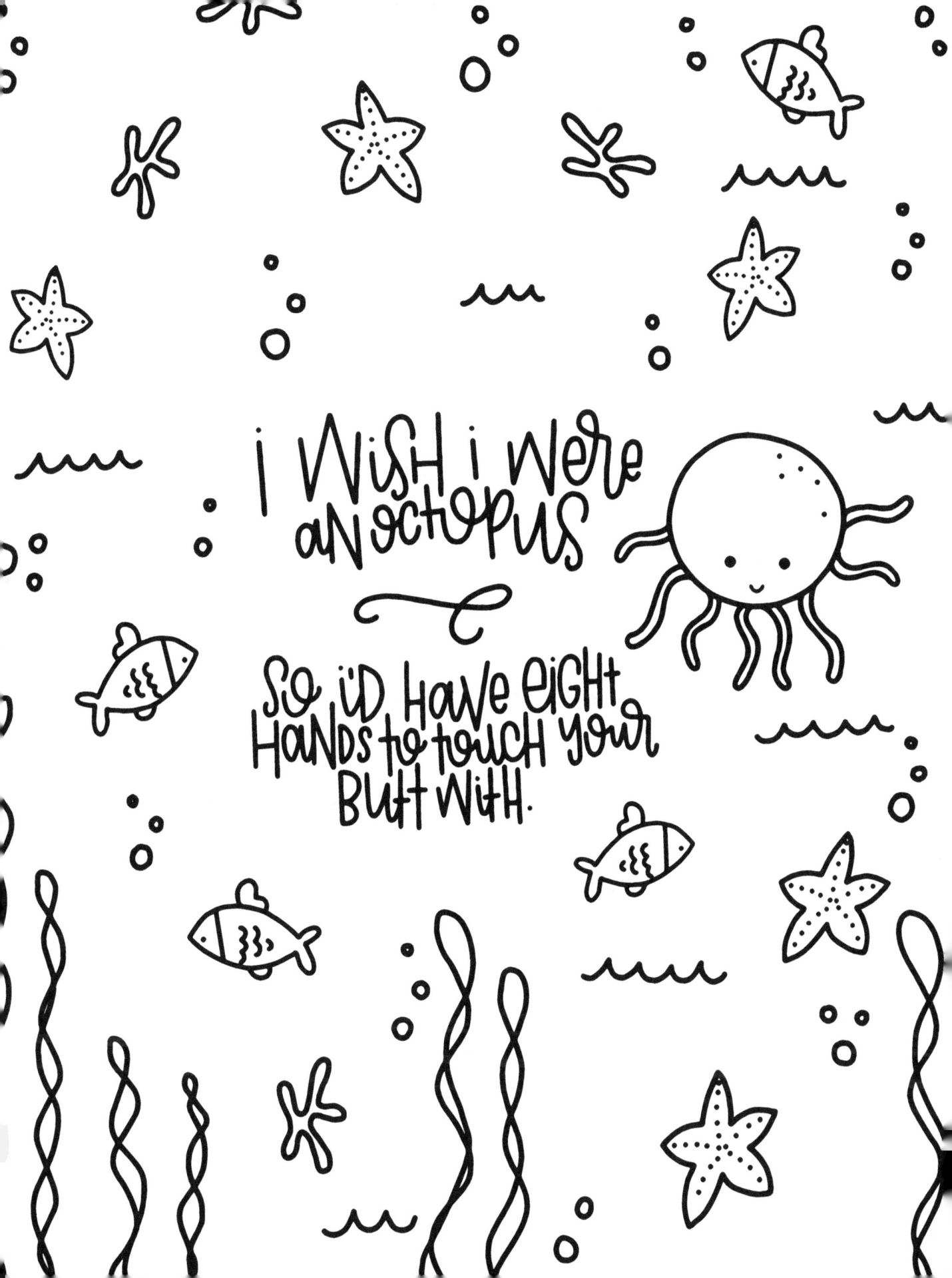

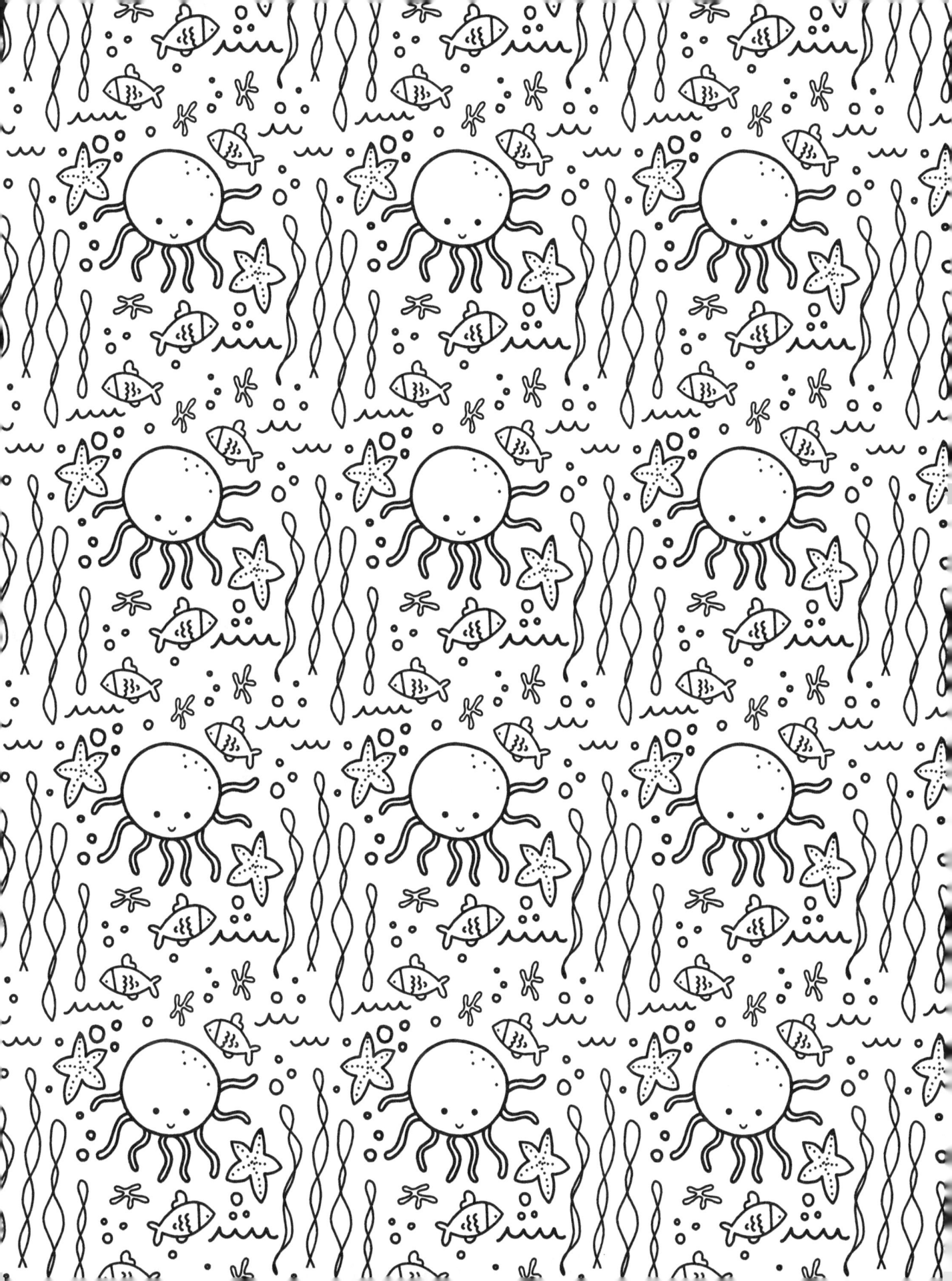

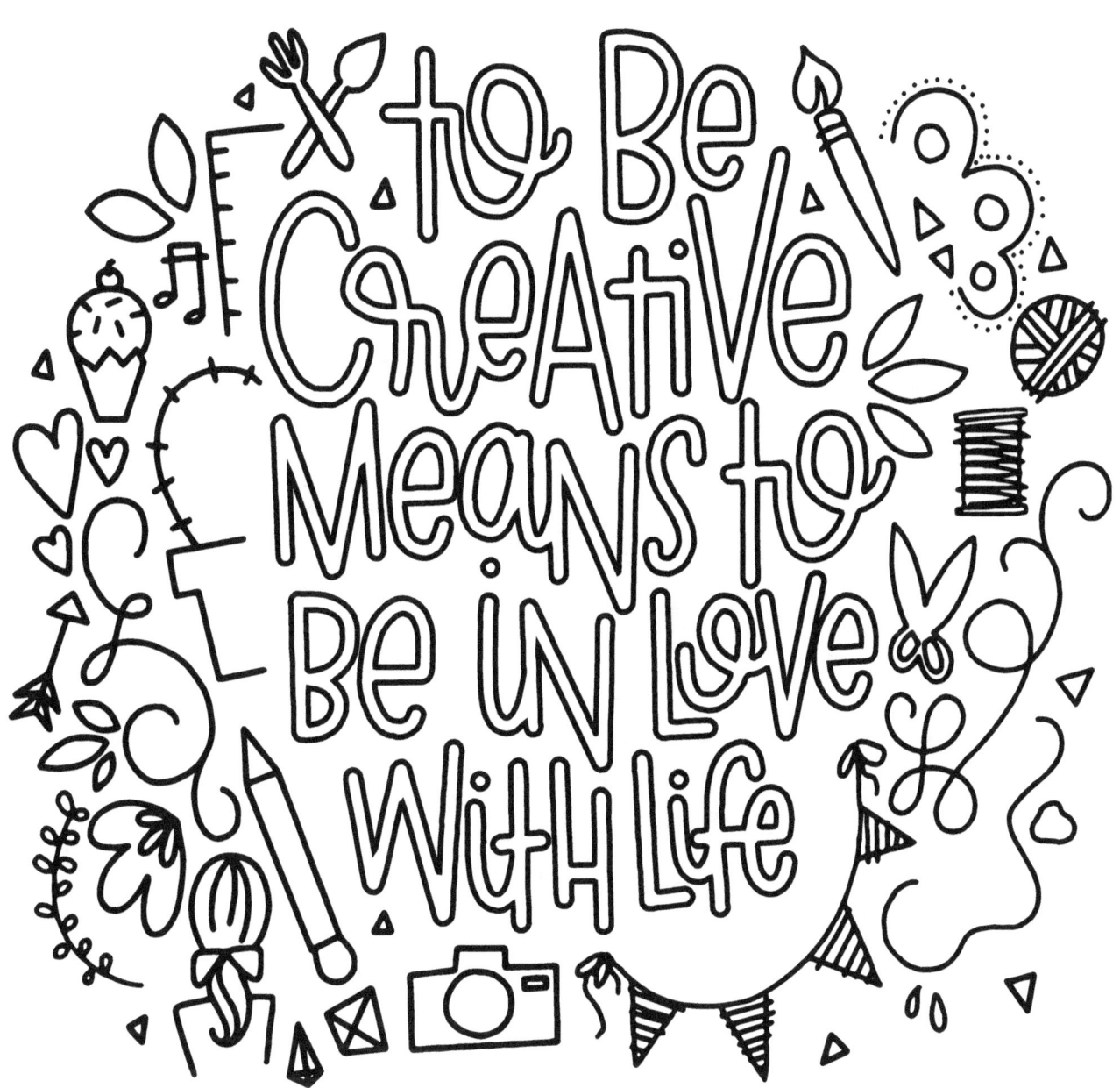

XOXO

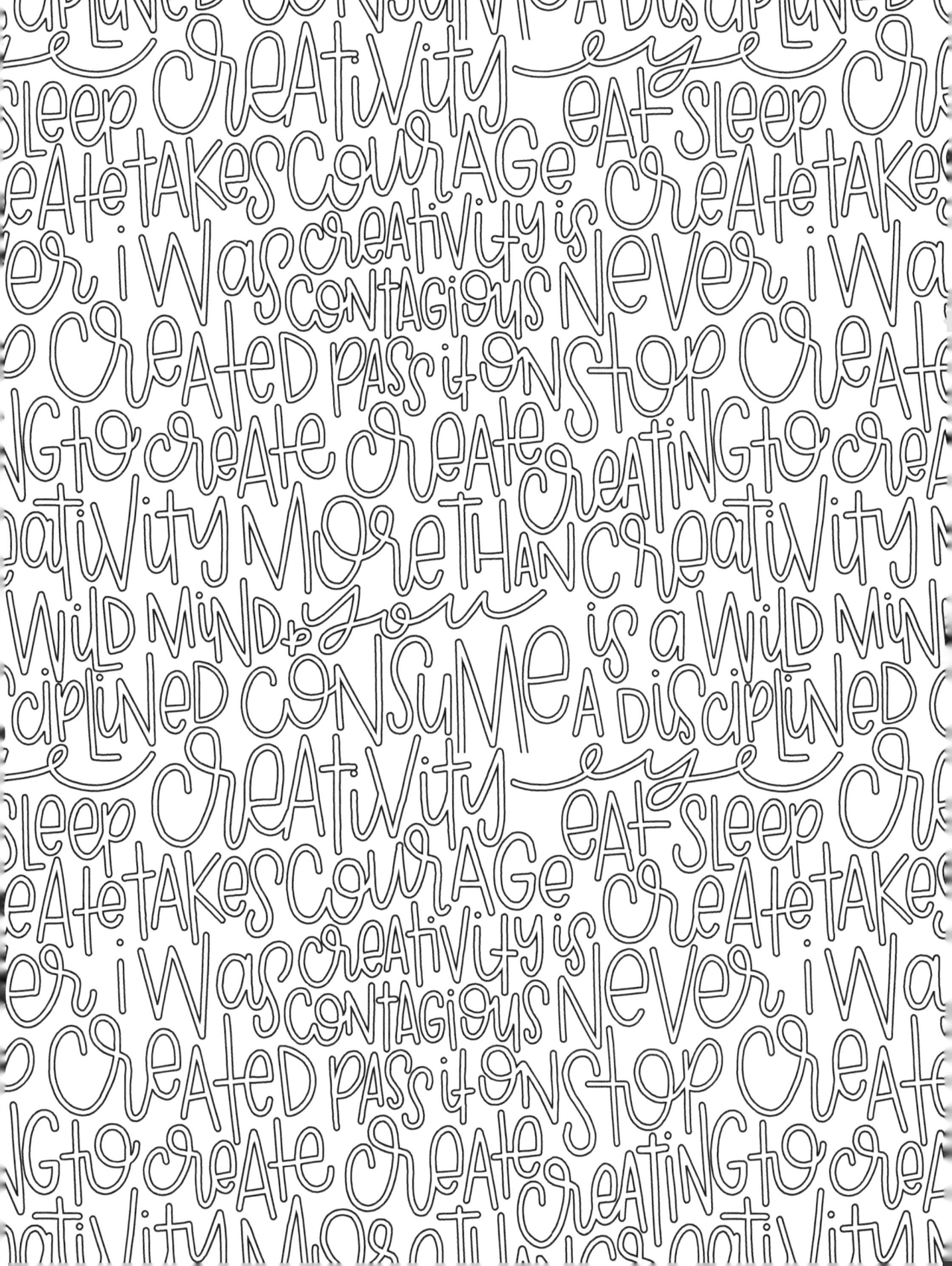